THE
PROGRAMMER'S
CRAFT

THE PROGRAMMER'S CRAFT:

Program Construction, Computer Architecture, and Data Management

RICHARD J. WEILAND

edited by Charles R. Bauer

RESTON PUBLISHING COMPANY, INC.
A Prentice-Hall Company
Reston, Virginia

Library of Congress Cataloging in Publication Data

Weiland, Richard J.
  The programmer's craft.

  Includes bibliographies.
    1. Electronic digital computers—Programming.
  2. Computer architecture. 3. Data structures.
  I. Bauer, Charles R.   II. Title.
  QA76.6.W436   1983   001.64'2   82-23018
  ISBN 0-8359-5645-8

Copyright 1983 by Reston Publishing Company, Inc.,
A Prentice-Hall Company, Reston, Virginia 22090

10 9 8 7 6 5 4 3 2 1

Printed in the United States of America.

To my son Jacob, who explained what was important, and to my wife Karen, who understood it all along.

CONTENTS

PREFACE

An interesting aspect of the way Rick Weiland writes and teaches is reflected in a recurrent remark from his students. Even when the lecture hall contained upwards of 200 people, students said, "I felt he was talking just to me."

The commitment to that kind of communication is apparent throughout this book, as it is in Rick's college teaching and, more recently, his well-regarded professional development workshops in Structured System Development. The explanations are cogent, the analogies are apt, and the examples are helpful. There is enough whimsy for entertainment without loss of substance.

In shaping the current version of this book, a number of goals were set. The first was that the book be independent of any particular computer or programming language, but be compatible with them all. This book will be useful in any computer environment. The choice of a programming language is up to the instructor.

The second was that it correspond well to a generally agreed on portion of the Computer Science curriculum. The book is aimed toward the material recommended by the Association for Computing Machinery for a second course in Computer Science.

The third, and by far the easiest as it turned out, was to make the book both substantive and entertaining. I think that Rick has succeeded very well on this count. A considerable number of the topics covered in this book are regarded as "hard" by students and teachers alike. However, I think you will find that the material is presented in such a natural and appealing way that you will be into, through, and comfortable with the material without ever having suspected that it was "hard."

A preliminary version of this book has been used for some years by the Illinois Institute of Technology's Computer Science Department. It has been successfully used by photographic arts majors and psychologists as well as by hundreds of budding Computer Scientists. Their reaction has uniformly been warm and I think yours will be too.

I am glad to share in this opportunity to let Rick Weiland talk just to you.

Charles R. Bauer
Illinois Institute of Technology
Chicago, Illinois

FOREWORD

By now you should already have had some exposure to computer programming and are ready to start exploring some of the theory and techniques that lie behind the programmer's craft. At least, that is where this book is aimed.

Some people using the book will be at the beginning of a career in data processing, or at least at the beginning of a computer science major. For these readers, I have tried to provide a broad introduction to the studies and the profession to come. The topics discussed will help to guide them in selecting further coursework and in picking a portion of the field to work in.

Others will use this book out of a side interest in data processing or simply because a course is required. I have tried to keep these readers in mind as well, since this book and the accompanying course may be the last formal exposure to data processing they will have. More and more, an intelligent understanding of what computers and computing are about is necessary to function effectively in our society, make reasonable decisions, and get our work done. My hope is that this book will promote this understanding.

For all readers, I hope I convey my *liking* for the subjects discussed. I find them interesting. I find them entertaining. I hope you can share in this feeling. Data processing, of course, is not everybody's cup of tea; but I hope it will not be anybody's cup of hemlock either.

I have tried to keep the tone of the book informal and easy to read. The mathematical rigor has been kept to a minimum in favor of advancing as many concepts as possible. At the same time, I have tried to tell the truth; there are no candy-coated generalities that you will have to unlearn later. I hope both the instructor and the student will find the topics covered thought-provoking and that they will be stimulated to go beyond the material covered directly. This puts some additional burden on the instructor to do some thinking before the teaching. However, I don't think the instructors I'm aiming for are going to find this much of a problem.

The book is arranged in three parts:

1. *Program Construction*: This part deals with the process by which programs get built. It is not so much concerned with the mechanics of

programming as with a constructive and craftsmanlike attitude toward programming. The primary topics are structured programming and bug control, with an emphasis on bug-preventive and defensive programming.

2. *Inside the Machine*: This part attempts to clear away some of the mystery that often accompanies a new acquaintance with computers, especially when the first exposure is via high-level languages. The topics address, in a conceptual way, what a computer does to execute a program and some of the steps through which a program moves en route from programming language to executable module.

3. *Nonnumeric Methods*: This part deals with a series of concepts and techniques that I find particularly interesting: the representation and manipulation of information and information structures. It includes chapters on the structures themselves, searching and sorting, and data management.

Originally, the book was written as a series of class notes, over a period of about 10 years, primarily to meet the teaching problems of the day. It was updated several times to incorporate advances in technology and changes in our culture. In retrospect, it is interesting to note that the three parts were written in essentially reverse order, although now they are certainly intended to be read in the order of presentation. Could this be a manifestation of stack-oriented thinking?

It is a pleasure to acknowledge the assistance and insight of the students and Computer Science faculty of the Illinois Institute of Technology who patiently suffered through several preliminary editions of the book and whose suggestions were invaluable. Particular thanks go to Professor Charles Bauer, for his unflagging belief that it all was publishable. I would also like to thank my friends and colleagues, past and present, at IIT, Yourdon, Inc., Improved System Technologies, Inc., Plum-Hall, Inc., and SEI, including: Tom Christopher, Jim Daniel, Ron Dougherty, Chris Gane, Joan Hall, Robert Kalke, Connie Knuth, Tim Lister, Michael Parks, Tom Plum, Krishnaiah Revuluri, Trish Sarson, Barbara Van Husen, Bob Walters, Bob Yeager, and Ed Yourdon; they have been unfailingly generous in sharing their insights and experience. My Reston reviewers, Fred Gruenberger, Pat Murphy, and Lloyd Weaver, were of great assistance in polishing the manuscript and in providing support and exceptionally constructive criticism. Particular thanks to Pat, whose suggestions have improved every chapter of this book. Thanks as well to SEI Information Technology for making the time and resources available for converting the notes into book form.

I cordially invite the sharp-eyed and quick-witted to seek out and advise me of any problems with this book, whether substantive or typographical. I know they're there, I wish they weren't. They are my responsibility, but I hope you will help me get rid of them. Advise me c/o SEI Information Technology, 450 East Ohio Street, Chicago, Illinois 60611, (312) 440-8300. Suitable rewards will obtain to the first discoverer of each problem.

A NOTE ON PROGRAMMING EXERCISES

One of the observations made in Chapter 2 is that programs are most readily built and tested through a well-structured team effort. However, one also observes that programming is made into a solitary task in many early Computer Science courses. (Primarily, I suppose, this is to allow grading based on individual achievement.)

Nonetheless, I want to encourage instructors of this material to establish team programming efforts (two to three members per team) including joint grades for programs, to the extent that such grades are necessary. I think this allows more sophisticated programs to be reasonably tackled and serves as a much more realistic introduction to professional data processing practice. Individual achievements can be reflected in activities better oriented to working alone (like examinations). I feel confident that the creative instructor will find ways to implement this modest proposal.

Richard J. Weiland

"Applicants for positions on university faculties or in industrial laboratories are usually asked about their proficiency in foreign languages. It is not unusual for this query to be given the answer, 'French, German, Fortran, and Algol.' . . . Such an answer is not flippancy; computer languages are foreign languages in a quite precise sense. Learning to use a digital computer is, more than anything else, learning to communicate with the computer by using one of these 'foreign' languages."

Anthony Ralston, *Introduction to Programming and Computer Science*

1

PROGRAM CONSTRUCTION

We are going to begin with two topics relating to the way people solve problems using computers. You know, of course, that we get computers to do things by writing a program. However, there is a lot of territory between the time a problem is first identified and the time that a working program is running to solve it. Part 1 focuses on a practical philosophy of program construction based on good sense and recent advances and discoveries in programming.

Structured programming deals with the way in which we translate ideas into effective, responsive programs. It provides mechanisms for making this process as accurate and understandable as possible, both for the original programmer and for later maintenance programmers, who accommodate the inevitable changes in program requirements.

Bug control is the process of keeping a program as free from errors as possible while it is being constructed, of removing any residual errors from a program as cleanly and quickly as possible, and of keeping the errors out as the program evolves over time. There are hard ways of effectively controlling bugs and easy ways. The easy ways, which we recommend, are mainly preventive, requiring a modest initial effort to save considerably greater trouble later on.

"How curiously it twists! It's more like a corkscrew than a path! . . . Well then, I'll try it the other way."

Lewis Carroll, *Through the Looking Glass,* Chapter 2

"I don't think they play at all fairly," Alice began, in rather a complaining tone . . . "and they don't seem to have any rules in particular: at least if there are, nobody attends to them—and you've no idea how confusing it is."

Lewis Carroll, *Alice in Wonderland,* Chapter 8

"I only said 'if'!" poor Alice pleaded. . . .

"But she said a great deal more than that!" the White Queen moaned. . . .

"So you did, you know," the Red Queen said to Alice. "Always speak the truth—think before you speak—and write it down afterwards."

Lewis Carroll, *Through the Looking Glass,* Chapter 11

1

STRUCTURED PROGRAMMING

1.1 "POWER CORRUPTS; ABSOLUTE POWER CORRUPTS ABSOLUTELY"

Hammers and saws are useful and versatile tools, but they can be used badly as well as skillfully. When tools are used badly, we get floors that sag and roofs that leak—houses that are difficult to maintain and unpleasant to live in. Computer programming languages are much the same. They are valuable tools for accomplishing a wide variety of tasks. But, in many cases, the tools are not applied skillfully or appropriately and the result is a programming system that leaks. It, too, is difficult to maintain and unpleasant to live with.

The subject of this chapter is the skillful use of programming languages through a series of techniques that have come to be called *structured programming*. The objective of structured programming is the development of programs that *work*, that are *clear and understandable*, and that are *easy to adjust* to evolving requirements.

The reason for this chapter is that, although programming languages have existed as tools for a long time, it is only recently that we have begun to understand the reasonable way to put them to use, to meet these objectives. In many ways, programming languages were a more powerful tool than we really knew how to control—filled with gadgets and gimmicks and interesting bells and whistles. Like the fabled Dr. Frankenstein, we used our less-than-adequate knowledge with good intentions, but with monsters as the results.

1.1.1 Old Heroes and New Heroes

When computers were small, slow, and expensive (relative to today's situation) and people were less costly than they are now, it made sense to have as a first priority that programs be as compact and quick-running as possible. The programming hero of the 1960s was the person who could write a program that was a little smaller and a little faster than the programmer down the block. The frequent result was a program that was a trifle more efficient, but also one that was more difficult to read and to change. An analogy might be a short story written without any vowels because we had only one sheet of paper. The sacrifice in clarity might have been worth the trouble, so that we could get the whole story onto that sheet.

Unlike short stories, programs are constantly being changed to accommodate new management information needs, or government regulations, or evolving business requirements. The importance of this fact may not be apparent in a classroom environment where, once a program is working, we hand it in or throw it away and generally have nothing much further to do with it. Out in the Real World, however, programs tend to have very long lives (often 10 years or longer) and go through many generations of change. In most data processing installations, better than half the annual budget is devoted to *program maintenance*—that is, the changing and adjusting of programs to meet new requirements. And several things have become true.

The first is that difficulty in understanding programs slows down the maintenance process: Before we can fix it, we have to understand what it is doing. In addition, in a program that is not cleanly written and constructed, the adjustments themselves tend to be messy. We have discovered that programs which were initially written to be small and fast at the expense of clarity didn't stay small and fast. As changes got made over the years, the programs grew into unwieldy mastodons—large and slow out of all proportion to the adjustments that were made.

The second is that computers have gotten larger, faster, and cheaper by several orders of magnitude. A home computer that you can buy now for the price of a good stereo system would have cost literally millions of dollars a few years ago. At the same time, the cost of people in data processing has gone up significantly.

A byproduct of the increase in computer power has been the development of increasingly sophisticated and complex programs, too complex to be handled by traditional system development tools. We can no longer afford to sacrifice clarity and understandability in programming for *any* consideration. Without them, the system doesn't get built right in the first place, and there is practically no hope of keeping it running successfully.

The new heroes, therefore, are the people who can write clear, understandable, maintainable programs that have long and successful lives with a minimum of fuss and bother. And it has turned out, in practically all cases, that clear, straightforward programs are quite efficient as well, not only fresh off the drawing boards, but over an extended period of time.

1.1.2   System Analysis and Design

A good deal of the process of building a successful large-scale system precedes the writing of code. There are two notable development stages that must be mentioned, although a full discussion is beyond the scope of this book.

The first is *system analysis* in which the problem to be solved is pinned down. This is often complicated by the fact that the person with the problem, the user, is not data processing oriented. The user is generally a business person or scientist who is faced with a difficulty in his or her own field: to get paychecks out on time, to forecast the weather, etc. The person delegated to develop the solution is often a data processing person who knows computers and programming, but who may only have a passing acquaintance with the business or scientific field in question. The job of system analysis is to bridge this gap for a particular problem without having to turn the user into a data processing expert or the systems person into a business/scientific application expert.

Once a problem is adequately defined, it will often be too large simply to sit down and solve by writing a program. By analogy, after determining that a bridge must be built across the Mississippi, we do not immediately grab a girder and welding torch and start construction. A large amount of organizational work remains, to define the major stages of the bridge-building process and to develop a piece by piece picture of the bridge to be constructed.

The process of *system design* breaks a large, unwieldy problem into a series of modest-sized pieces (usually through several stages) each of which *can* be solved and assembled into an overall solution to the problem. The trick is to generate pieces that have the simplest possible interfaces so that putting the pieces back together again correctly does not represent a more formidable problem than we started with.

While this may seem like a lot of problem-solving machinery, the stages described are absolutely essential for large-scale systems, which may end up comprising tens of thousands of lines of program code.

We will look at a very modest part of system design that can be of immediate assistance in developing reasonable programs. Then we will focus on the process of writing program code for a modest-sized program or for a modest-sized, well-defined piece of a larger program.

1.2 TOP-DOWN DESIGN

Top-down design is the general process of going from a large, complicated problem to a series of smaller problems, each of which has a greater probability of being solvable than the original problem. Another way of saying the same thing is that we want to understand a complex system in terms of its subsystems. This takes some care, in dividing things up, to make sure that the pieces are simpler than the original system. For example, if we were to simply slice an automobile into two-foot cross sections, the pieces would be physically smaller but conceptually messier than the entire car taken as a functional whole.

1.2.1   Black Boxes

One desirable characteristic of the system pieces or *modules* is that they take the form of black boxes. A *black box* is a module that can be understood solely in terms of *what* it does (its function), the data it needs in order to do its job (its inputs), and the results it produces (its outputs). In particular, we do not need to know *how* a black box goes about its job in order to understand it. To take a classic example, consider a square root subroutine. To understand and use the routine we need to know what it does (calculate a square root), what it needs (a nonnegative number), and what it produces (the square root of the input value). But we do *not* need to know how the routine works. It might calculate a square root by using Newton's method, a Taylor series, logarithms, or a table lookup. As long as the routine works faithfully, we don't need to know *how* it works to make good use of the routine. We will diagram a black box like this:

with the routine's name inside the box, a large arrow pointing down to indicate that the routine is called from the outside, and small arrows indicating the movement of data to and from the black box (i.e., its inputs and outputs).

1.2.2   Structure Charts

Part of the importance of having simple, self-contained black box modules is that we can use the black boxes to understand the function of the higher-level module that calls on our black boxes. Thus, if our main task was to make a layer cake, we could understand the process of making the cake in terms of its subordinate black boxes:

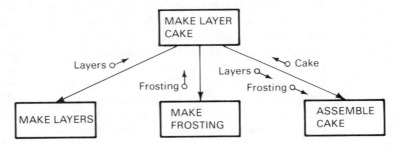

If we are just superficial observers, this may be enough of a description of the cake-making process to satisfy us. If we are striving for the Cordon Bleu, however, we will probably be interested in more detail. For example, we might want to understand MAKE LAYERS in terms of *its* subordinate modules:

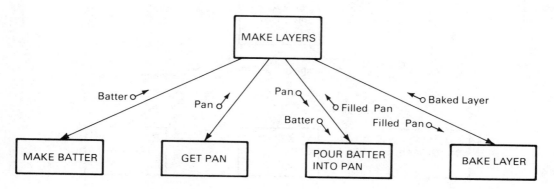

This can get carried out to as many levels of detail as needed to fully specify the process. A pleasant thing about black box top-down design is that we can parcel out work. We could have one designer working on the details of MAKE BATTER and another working on the details of BAKE LAYER. As long as there is a mutual agreement on *what* is being done and on the meanings of the information flowing around the system (the little arrows), the designers can work independently. In fact, it could be the case that our large process, MAKE LAYER CAKE, is really just a subordinate module of the larger process PLAN A BIRTHDAY PARTY. Note that we can go ahead and specify MAKE LAYER CAKE and indeed carry out the necessary steps to make the cake, independent of all of the other activities involved in planning a party. This is a very helpful feature for building large systems—if everybody had to know, in detail, what everybody else was doing, nothing would ever get accomplished.

The diagram we have been using is called a *structure chart* or *hierarchy chart*. It displays the interrelationships between modules of a system. It shows which modules are called on by which other modules and how information moves through the system (see Figure 1.1).

1.2.3 The Hitch

The problem with top-down design is that it is not always easy to do, although most people can do some of it. The most difficult part of top-down design is deciding how to break down a module into subordinate parts; that is, deciding what the reasonable subdivisions are. It is not unusual, particularly for the novice, to put reasonable submodules in unreasonable places. One question that should be asked frequently is the top-down question. In looking at a lower-level module, ask, "Does this module contribute to the job of the calling module? Is it a necessary

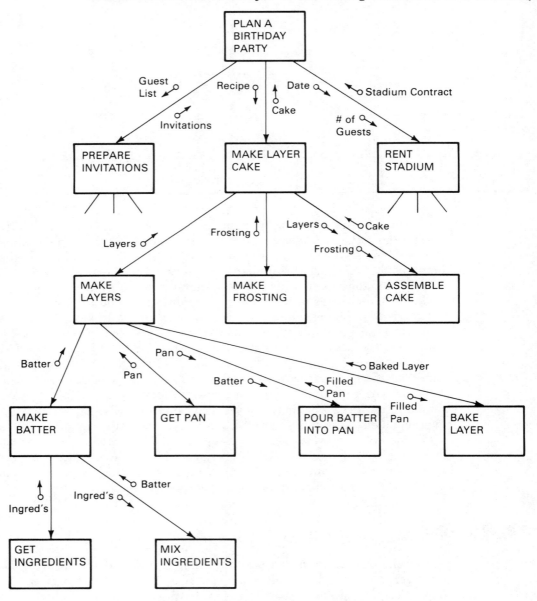

FIGURE 1.1   Partial Structure Chart for *Plan a Birthday Party*.

subpart of the calling module?" If the answer is yes, the submodule is probably properly placed.

1.3   STRUCTURED CODING

The techniques of structured coding are directed at the writing of program code that accomplishes the job of a module in the structure chart. This implies, obviously, that the development of a structure chart should *precede* the writing of any code. Here, we are primarily concerned with the executable code that directs the computer to *do* something, not the declarative code that primarily describes the way data looks inside the computer's memory. Executable code is broadly divided into two classifications: data manipulations and control structures.

1.3.1   Data Manipulations

Data manipulations are the basic nuts and bolts of any programming language, the instructions that actually do the work. Data manipulations include statements for doing calculations, copying information from one place in memory to another, input, output, etc. Data manipulation statements are easy to deal with logically, because each one is basically self-contained. If we wanted to diagram* a data manipulation statement, we could simply place it into a rectangle, to emphasize its self-containedness:

```
Calculate A ← B + C
```

1.3.2   Control Structures

Control structures are the parts of a program that specify what is to be done next. They specify the order in which the statements that compose a program are to be executed, in effect directing traffic among the program's statements.

The main contribution of structured coding is to observe: (a) that some control structures are self-contained the way data manipulations are and some are not and (b) that sticking to the self-contained control structures promotes program clarity and maintainability. The primary

---

*Diagramming conventions are based on the work of Nassi and Shneiderman [8].

examples of self-contained control structures are simple sequence, if-else, repetition, and case. (Don't worry if not all these names are familiar to you; they go by various designations in various programming languages. Once you see how they operate, it should be pretty clear how you do them in *your* programming language.)

1.3.3 Simple Sequence

The simplest control structure is almost invisible. In the absence of directions to the contrary, the computer simply goes from one statement to the next, in sequence. Consequently, if we diagram two data manipulations, one after the other:

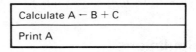

it is understood that we mean that the first manipulation is to be done, immediately followed by the second. Obviously, we can string together as many small rectangles as we want to build a larger routine. We can also draw a super-rectangle around the whole sequence. Simple sequence is about as self-contained as you can get.

1.3.4 Repetition

The most common nonsequential thing that a program or computer does is to repeat some operation (or series of operations) over and over again. This might be stepping through a table, or processing a series of student records, or printing the individual lines of a telephone directory, etc. The structure that corresponds to this kind of repetition is called a *loop*. Other names for this structure are Repeat-While, Do-While, Perform-Until, and even others in various programming languages. Regardless of name, a repetition basically contains two parts: an operation (or sequence of operations) to be repeated (called the *scope*) and a *condition* that tells us when to stop repeating. We can diagram a repetition as:

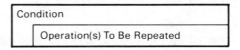

Note that the scope forms a rectangle or rectangle stack and that the entire repetition structure is a single rectangle (i.e., it is itself self-contained). As an example, suppose we had a table called ACCOUNTS, with ACCOUNT-MAX rows, and that we wanted to place a zero into each table slot. We could invent a counter called ACCOUNT-POINTER that will point to successive table slots, and diagram:

ACCOUNT-POINTER ← 1	(1)
While ACCOUNT-POINTER ≤ ACCOUNT-MAX	(2)
ACCOUNTS (ACCOUNT-POINTER) ← 0	(3)
ACCOUNT-POINTER ← ACCOUNT-POINTER + 1	(4)

The effect of this loop is to place zeros in successive slots of ACCOUNTS, until the counter gets larger than the table size. This simple loop displays all of the typical features of most repetition structures in context: Line (1) is an initialization, setting up the starting environment for the repetition to operate. Line (2) is the condition part of the repetition proper. Lines (3) and (4) are the scope, but line (4) is notable in that it serves the function of getting the environment ready for the *next* iteration. This function is usually called *increment* even if no number is being changed.

An important feature of repetition structures in most (though not all) languages is that the repetition is done *zero* or more times, depending on condition. That is, if we hit a repetition structure and the terminating condition is already satisfied, the loop scope is not executed even once. In the example above, if ACCOUNTS was a degenerate table with no rows (i.e., ACCOUNT-MAX = 0), then the condition on line (2) would be immediately satisfied (since ACCOUNT-POINTER would be greater than ACCOUNT-MAX) and the scope would be skipped. The program would proceed on to whatever actions followed the repetition structure.

1.3.5 IF-ELSE

Next most common is the IF-ELSE structure in which a true-false question is asked and one of two mutually exclusive sets of operations is performed, depending on the answer to the question. We diagram the IF-ELSE as:

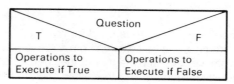

As before, the sets of operations are themselves rectangles or rectangle stacks, and the entire IF-ELSE structure is a rectangle. As an example, suppose we have just completed a data validation process that starts with ERROR-FLAG equal to zero, but which sets ERROR-FLAG to one if any error is detected. We now want to print out an appropriate message:

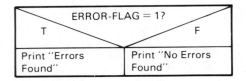

A generalization of the IF-ELSE is the *case* structure which chooses among several mutually exclusive sets of operations rather than just two. Some languages have a built-in case structure. For those that do not, the case is easy to build from multiple IF-ELSE structures (see Figure 1.2).

	Case of STATE-CODE
IL	Things to do when STATE-CODE = 'IL'
WI	Things to do when STATE-CODE = 'WI'
IN	Things to do when STATE-CODE = 'IN'
	Things to do when STATE-CODE is none of the above

In languages that do not support a CASE statement directly, this kind of structure is typically written as:

```
IF STATE-CODE = 'IL'
    ('IL' processing)
ELSE
IF STATE-CODE = 'WI'
    ('WI' processing)
ELSE
IF STATE-CODE = 'IN'
    ('IN' processing)
ELSE
    (default processing)
```

FIGURE 1.2   The CASE Structure

The CASE structure is used for multi-way decision making—when one processing alternative is to be selected from a series of mutually exclusive possibilities. Note the existence (and importance) of the "default bucket" which provides a processing alternative when none of the tested choices is correct.

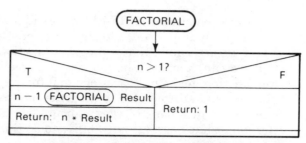

FIGURE 1.3   Factorial (Recursive)

while we're winding our way down to the safety net. The main problem is that we're liable to run out of space to hold status information, even for a fairly straightforward recursive calculation.

You should certainly keep recursion available in your programming tool kit, but don't expect it to work miracles for you.

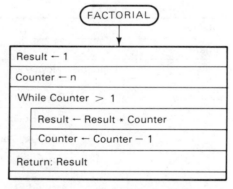

FIGURE 1.4   Factorial (Iterative)

1.3.7   Nesting

This completes our basic repertoire of self-contained control structures. Their most important feature is that each of them has the same "shape," namely that of a rectangle. There are two primary reasons why this similarity of shape is important.

First, the similarity means that we can enclose (or *nest*) structures within one another to any extent we desire, to build a program sophisticated enough to handle any application. Thus, it is not surprising to find IF-ELSEs within the scope of a repetition or an invocation as one of the operations under an IF-ELSE (see Figure 1.5).

Equally important, the similarity of shape promotes maintainability. If we determine that a program function must be altered, we know that we can "unplug" the module implementing the current version of the function, make modifications to it (perhaps rewrite the function completely), and still be able to plug the new version back in without any dangling connections to worry about. The fact that all structures have the same shape assures our ability to do this.

1.3.8 The GOTO

There is a remaining control structure that must be mentioned, namely the unconditional branch or GOTO. The function of this structure in most

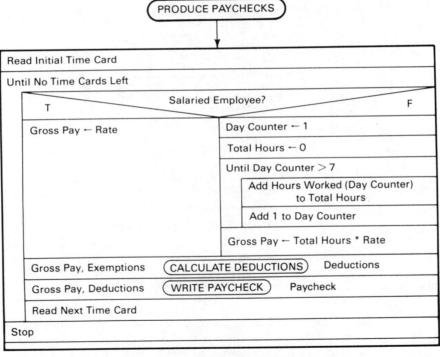

FIGURE 1.5   A Structured Flowchart

The routine diagrammed accepts a series of time cards and generates a corresponding series of paychecks. Salaried employees are paid a fixed gross salary. Hourly workers' gross is determined by summing the hours they worked each day and multiplying the sum by an hourly rate. In both cases, after determining gross, deductions are calculated and a check is written.

programming languages is to direct the computer to continue execution from a different (named) place in the program. The problem with the GOTO is that it is *not* self-contained. It simply sends control off into the blue with no guarantee of return. Programs with many GOTOs in them tend to be hard to follow, since each time we encounter a GOTO we must mark our place and trace after it. (With an invocation, we can assume, at least for the moment, that an invoked routine *does* its job and returns.) Programs that make heavy use of GOTOs represent a lot of place marking and a lot of potential confusion.

In some circles, eradicating GOTOs is considered synonymous with structured programming. This is misleading. Programs can certainly still be badly written even if they have no GOTOs. However, it *is* possible to write programs without GOTOs in most current high-level languages (Fortran '77, ANS Cobol, PL/I, Pascal) and doing so is often an illuminating exercise. In general, we will say that intelligently constructed, thoughtfully designed programs will tend to need very few GOTOs, and that a proliferation of GOTOs in any high-level language program is frequently indicative of poor programming habits. The example programs shown throughout this book do entirely without GOTOs.

1.4   PROGRAMMING STYLISTICS

There are a number of other good general rules of thumb that fall into the general realm of sensible program construction. They are not part of structured programming per se, but work well together with its concepts.

1.4.1   Format Code Sensibly

Program readability is greatly promoted by the sensible arrangement of program code on the printed or hand-written page. Some general rules that have been widely accepted are:

- Write a maximum of one statement per line. If a statement won't all fit on a line, indent its continuation (say four spaces).
- Indent the statements under control of IF-ELSE to highlight the control structure.
- Start each new module at the top of a new page.

1.4.2   Keep Module Sizes Reasonable

There is considerable agreement that an invoked module should not be much longer than one page of code. This corresponds nicely to about a page of structured flowchart. Think of a box on a structure chart (e.g., Figure 1.1) as representing about a page of code.

At the other end, it is a good idea to avoid a multitude of teensy modules. In some cases, a module just a few lines long is reasonable or may be required by the syntax of the programming language. However, a great many modules smaller than 10 lines long will tend to complicate life rather than simplify it.

1.4.3   Don't Be Cryptic

To the extent that your programming language permits, use readable, meaningful names for data and procedures. Readable and meaningful does not necessarily mean lengthy. While names like X and SW1 are singularly nonilluminating, long similar names like GOOD-CUS-TOMER-NAME-SPECIFICATION   and   GOOD-CUSTOMER-ADDR-SPECIFICATION can cloud the issue also, if overdone, and cause writers cramp. Make sure names are distinct (e.g., GCS-NAME, GCS-ADDRESS).

Avoid general data items that are used for multiple purposes. The use of a variable for more than one purpose will inevitably introduce bugs and make maintenance more difficult. If you need a new variable, devise one; don't reuse an old one.

1.4.4   Be Obvious

Remember when writing a program that you are writing for someone else to read. Cleverness at the expense of clarity is a very poor trade-off. Avoid side effects of a language (that is, the use of a statement to accomplish jobs other than the one for which it was intended, via quirks in the way the statement operates).

Make judicious use of meaningful comments. The most useful comment is a one sentence description of the function or purpose of a module, appearing at the module's beginning. The least useful comment is one that repeats the code without explaining anything:

```
A = A + 1; ( (increase A by 1) )
```

Even less useful is a comment that is wrong or misleading. Avoid these, too, of course.

1.4.5 The Process-Read Loop

We make a special point about one particular kind of repetition because it occurs with great frequency in many programming applications and because, in practice, it is often constructed inappropriately.

One of the most common activities in data processing is to read and process a sequence of records*, one at a time. This is commonly programmed as shown in Figure 1.6. There are a number of problems with this implementation.

First, we are actually making two end-of-file tests for each iteration of the loop. We are not concerned with the execution time this wastes, which is insignificant, but rather with a potential maintenance problem: if our end-of-file check needs maintenance, we now have to make fixes in two different places instead of just one.

More important, there is a design unattractiveness about the loop scope. Rather than simply carrying out its prime responsibility (process a record), it gives us an argument. "Should I *really* process the record . . . Well, let me see if I feel like it." This sounds a bit whimsical, but really has considerable underlying importance from the program design viewpoint. We should not ask a routine to process a record when none is left.

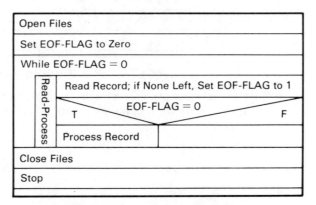

FIGURE 1.6   Read-Process Loop

A common, but unnecessarily complex mechanism for processing a series of records. Its primary problem is incorrect loop initialization, causing the need for excessively complex logic later.

---

*A *record* is a chunk of information for processing. Interesting data processing tasks often involve a lengthy series of similar records. Examples are grade slips to be applied to student records, the student records themselves, employee timecards for payroll processing, etc. We'll discuss this at length in Chapter 7.

The real problem here is that this program does not genuinely correspond to our basic four-part loop structure of initialization, condition, scope, and increment. In particular, the initialization is missing. The way this program *should* look is shown in Figure 1.7 in which each of the repetition parts is marked.

The place where programmers have gone astray over the years is that, by coincidence, the initialization part and the increment part of the read-and-process loop turned out to be the same line of code. And, because programmers are intrinsically lazy, they avoided writing that line more than once. Unfortunately, the short-term laziness has led to enormous problems in program construction and maintenance. We argue here for longer term laziness: Write programs to save the maximum amount of trouble in the *long* run. (Note that even in the short run, the properly constructed program is really simpler than the old version.)

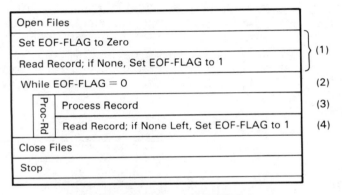

FIGURE 1.7   Process-Read Loop

A more sensible way of constructing the loop to process a series of records. The four basic parts of a standard loop are marked: (1) initialization, (2) condition, (3) scope, (4) increment.

1.5   PREPARING TO MEET THE REAL WORLD

With some practice on your part, we hope you will agree that structured programming is a sensible way of building programs and that you will develop good programming habits based on the guidelines provided. There are a couple of warnings, however, to which you are entitled.

1.5.1   Structured Programming Is Not a Religion

Programming is still a craft, not a science or a religion. We have presented a series of guidelines that have worked well for many people over a number of years. However, guidelines do not have the force of natural laws, religious laws, or statute. There will be a number of circumstances that represent exceptions to the general rules. A blind adherence to guidelines in the face of overwhelming contrary evidence is not sensible.

Historically, this has led to some problems. The "no GOTO" guideline became a religion for some programmers, even when their programming language did not support enough self-contained control structures to solve problems conveniently. As a consequence, the guidelines did not always work very well and the religious fanatics, having been disappointed by their faith, rejected all of structured programming. This is an understandable, but unfortunate overreaction.

The other side of the coin, however, is that if you are new to structured programming, you may run into situations that *look* like exceptions to the guidelines, but really can be readily solved within them if you look at the problem the right way. Consequently, we suggest that you talk potential exceptions over with other programmers to see whether the situation is a real exception. You will probably find, with practice, that there are fewer exceptions than you thought.

1.5.2   Rome Isn't Rebuilt in a Day

There are a great many running programs out in the Real World that are not structured. As structured programming becomes more widely accepted, the percentage of *newly* written programs that are structured continues to increase. However, the longevity of programs means that many unstructured programs will be with us for a long time. If you have to work with unstructured programs, you will very rapidly appreciate the value of self-contained control structures. However, you should also be prepared to cope with code that is less than attractive. A frequently reasonable strategy is to rewrite modest portions of a program that requires maintenance, to introduce structuring at least in the vicinity of the needed change. However, do not take it upon yourself to rewrite a whole program unless someone has expressed a willingness to pay for the effort.

1.6   SUMMARY

We have tried to present the basic concepts and tools of structured programming. Like other aspects of programming and other skill areas (such as bicycle riding or playing a clarinet), the only real way to appreciate what's going on is to put the tools into practice. We expect you to find, as others have, that structured programming increases your feeling of craftsmanship and satisfaction with your work, as well as increasing the quality of the product you produce.

EXERCISES

Terms You Should Know . . .

Arguments	Nesting
Black Box	Program Maintenance
CASE Structure	Recursion
Control Structure	Repetition
GOTO	Simple Sequence
IF-ELSE	Structure Chart
Increment	Structured Flowchart
Invocation	System Analysis
Iterative	System Design
Module	Top-Down

1. Starting from the information given in Figure 1.1, provide the next level of top-down design for the module called PREPARE INVITATION. Be sure to show the flow of information.

2. Which of the two structure chart segments below actually represents part of a top-down design? Explain your choice. Fill in the information flows.

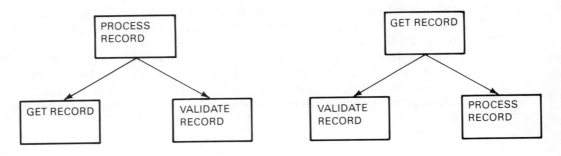

3. Draw a segment of structured flowchart for a loop that is to be executed *one* or more times. That is, for example, PROCESS ITEM is to be repeated until COND-1 becomes true, but even if COND-1 is initially true, PROCESS ITEM is to be executed one time.

4. Draw a segment of structured flowchart showing a three-way decision, for example executing LESS ROUTINE if A < B, EQUAL ROUTINE if A = B, and MORE ROUTINE if A > B.

5. Draw a structured flowchart for a process that reads two streams of numbers (each stream in ascending order) and that prints the numbers which appear in both streams (but not in just one of the streams).

6. Assume that the code shown below is a complete program and that the called routines will be supplied separately. Translate this code into new code which observes our guidelines and which contains no GOTOs. The names shifted to the left are labels. Assume that the scopes of IFs are terminated by a semicolon. Comment on the original code and your results.

```
        IF A = B GO TO L5;
        IF B = C GO TO L6;
L1.
        CALL R1;
        GO TO L5;
L2.
        CALL R2;
        GO TO L6;
L3.
        CALL R3;
L4.
        IF D = E GO TO L3 ELSE GO TO L7;
L5.
        CALL R4;
        GO TO L7;
L6.
        CALL R5;
        GO TO L1;
L7.
        CALL R6;
L8.
        STOP;
```

7. Draw a structured flowchart for each of the following situations. Each is a repetition that steps through a table T and sets RESULT to 'FOUND' if its search condition is met, to 'LOST' otherwise. Search conditions are:

a. Any slot of T contains a 1.
b. All slots of T contain 1.
c. At least two slots of T contain 1.
d. Exactly two slots of T contain 1.
e. Any two *consecutive* slots of T contain 1.

8. Explain why the use of a GOTO conflicts with structured programming? What specific concepts of structured programming are violated by the GOTO? Under what circumstances might the use of a GOTO still be a good idea?

9. What, if anything, is wrong with the following diagrammed program fragment?

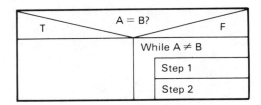

10. The Fibonacci numbers are a series where each new term is the sum of the previous two terms: 1, 1, 2, 3, 5, 8, 13, ...

$$F(1) = 1, F(2) = 1$$
$$F(k) = F(k-1) + F(k-2), \text{ for } k > 2.$$

Write structured flowcharts or programs that implement $F(k)$ returning the kth Fibonacci number:
a. Recursively
b. Iteratively

11. Suppose we had a computer that supported addition and subtraction but not multiplication or division. We could define a MULT function for multiplication, by noting that

$$n \times m = ((n-1) + 1) \times ((m-1) + 1), \text{ for } n, m > 0$$
$$= (n-1)(m-1) + (n-1) + (m-1) + 1$$

and $n \times m = 0$, for n or $m = 0$

a. Write the recursive formula for multiplication using this definition and write a structured flowchart or program that implements it.

b. Write a structured flowchart or program to implement multiplication iteratively.

12. Using the same assumptions as in Exercise 11, devise a definition for division that uses only addition and/or subtraction for arithmetic operations. Then:

    a. Implement your definition recursively as a structured flowchart or program.

    b. Implement it iteratively.

13. Define n# (read "n termial") as the sum of the integers from 1 to n.

    a. Write recursive and iterative definitions of n#.

    b. Write programs that calculate 1,000,000# iteratively and recursively and compare the results.

    c. What's a better way of calculating this result than either an iterative or recursive calculation?

"You should say what you mean," the March Hare went on.

"I do," Alice hastily replied; "at least I mean what I say—that's the same thing, you know."

"Not the same thing a bit!" said the Hatter. "Why you might just as well say that 'I see what I eat' is the same as 'I eat what I see'!"

Lewis Carroll, Alice in Wonderland, Chapter 7

"Would you tell me, please," said Alice, a little timidly, "why you are painting those roses?" . . .

"Why, the fact is, you see, Miss, this here ought to have been a *red* rosetree, and we put a white one in by mistake; and if the Queen was to find it out, we should all have our heads cut off . . ."

Lewis Carroll, Alice in Wonderland, Chapter 8

"What sort of insects do you rejoice in, where *you* come from?" the Gnat inquired.

"I don't rejoice in insects at all," Alice explained.

Lewis Carroll, Through the Looking Glass, Chapter 3

"My programs have fewer bugs, because I put fewer in."

Robert B. K. Dewar

2

BUG CONTROL

2.1 INTRODUCTION

In *Anna Karenina*, Tolstoy wrote: "All happy families are happy in the same way. Each unhappy family is unhappy in its own way." A similar (if not so profound) observation can be made about programs. In a sense, happily working programs all have a similar, robust feel to them. In contrast, programs that don't work are nonworking each in their own peculiar fashion. Because of this peculiarity, *bug control,* the process of getting and keeping errors out of programs, tends to be more of an art form than a science.

In a sense, trying to teach an art form in a book is silly. However, some useful observations can be made.

2.1.1 Even Art Forms Have Rules

In the first place, teaching the rudiments of an art is certainly possible, including its mechanics and a basic appreciation for How It's Done. This does not produce many new Old Masters (unless the talent was already there) but it *can* help to develop competent craftsmen. That's what we are shooting for in this chapter.

2.1.2 Bugs Are Errors, Not Organisms

Second, we call our programming errors "bugs" as though, like viruses or germs, they had an independent existence in the universe. We like to think that bugs arise spontaneously, creeping into our programs like mites into old flour and that programs will contain bugs no matter what precautions we take. That takes some of the psychological heat away from creating programs that don't work: It's not *our* fault . . . bugs just happen!

The fact is, of course, that *bugs are mistakes* and we made them. There are two basic approaches we can take to producing bug-free programs: Take some initial trouble to prevent bugs from getting into our programs in the first place, or take (typically) a lot more trouble to get them out later. In practice, we're probably going to have to do some of both.

2.1.3 Kinds of Bugs

Let's start by noting that there are at least three kinds of bugs.

Worst is the *specification bug,* a misunderstanding between the person who commissions a program and the person who builds it. The reason that this kind of bug is worst is that it is often not discovered until a program is finished and, when discovered, it may require massive rewrites of major portions of the code. A specification bug means we've "solved" the wrong problem. In the classroom, this is a nuisance. In industry, it may represent the waste of hundreds of thousands of dollars plus significant delays in making vitally needed systems operational.

Second worst is the *interface bug* in which there is a misunderstanding among the pieces of the program on how things are supposed to fit together. Interface bugs include a mismatch in conventions between a routine and the program that calls it, or a disagreement between a program's READ statement and the way the input data actually looks, or the execution of a loop too many times (or too few), or the inadvertent misstatement of a condition in a test or loop control (e.g., saying "less than" when you meant "less than or equal to"), etc.

What makes this kind of bug difficult to fix is that the error is often far removed from the evidence of trouble. For example, we may get a "negative argument" error return from a square root routine when the real problem is that we misstated the length of an input data item and read some character data as though it were numeric. Tracking the apparent problem down to the actual problem is often very tricky.

Least severe, but most common, is the *calculation bug* where we simply goofed: we wrote 2 where we meant 1, or + where we meant −, or left something out. These bugs are no fun, of course, but they are easiest to fix since the apparent problem in results is fairly easily traced to the actual error.

We omit from further consideration *syntax bugs,* in which we write (or enter) a program statement that the translator recognizes as incorrectly constructed. These occur with embarrassing frequency, alas, but most language translators these days provide excellent diagnostics and the fixes are straightforward.

The bug/germ comparison was a metaphor, of course, not a biological fact of life, and some uses of the metaphor have been unconstructive. However, we can exploit the metaphor to draw some parallels between successful programming and successful medicine, both preventive and curative, and derive some useful insights and techniques along the way.

2.2 PREVENTIVE MEDICINE: BUG-PREVENTIVE PROGRAMMING

The old proverb, "An ounce of prevention is worth a pound of cure," applies as well to the development of computer programs as it does elsewhere. However, the ounce of prevention only works if we do it and too often we don't. (Maybe a metric version of the proverb would sound more scientific and convincing.) The difficulty in applying the proverb is twofold.

First, we tend to kid ourselves. Thinking that "nothing will go wrong this time" seems to be one of the primary delusions of our species. Everyone (particularly computer programmers) ought to know by now that "nothing will go wrong" is the rare exception not the rule—but that's what delusions are all about. We hope that by mentioning the delusion one more time, we will at least increase your consciousness of it a little.

Second, as observed in the last chapter, we like to be lazy, although we're often not very good at it. Constructive laziness (which we recommend) tries to minimize overall, long-term effort. This typically involves taking a small amount of additional up-front care (the ounce of prevention) to save large amounts of trouble later. On the other hand, unconstructive laziness minimizes short-term effort, but often at the expense of large amounts of later effort (the pound of cure).

Is there any hope? By understanding the *process* of bug-preventive programming we can get a better handle on how to be constructively lazy, and with such a handle be more inclined to take the small amount of necessary up-front trouble.

2.2.1   Aseptic Programming

The best way to prevent infection, say in a surgical environment, is not to let germs get anywhere near the site of the operation. This is aseptic medicine. How do we keep bugs away from our programming site?

2.2.1.1   User Feedback   The best way to prevent specification bugs is to maintain a high and effective level of communication between the program specifier and the program builder. This is one of the primary functions of system analysis, as mentioned earlier. A smart system analyst begins by listening carefully to the user's (or instructor's) requirements, but does not stop there. Good analysis must also include asking relevant questions, getting clarifications where necessary, and *feeding back* our understanding of those requirements.

An important part of building this understanding is to carefully separate *what* the user needs to have done from *how* we are going to meet these needs. Remember that a Real World user, say a payroll manager, does not really care whether paychecks are created by a computer system or by little green trolls on high stools—provided the work is done accurately, economically, and on time. It's up to us to determine first what the user *means* by "accurately, economically, and on time" and worry later about the effective means to provide the service. As computer people, we will probably have more interest in computer systems than troll systems, but the first step is the same regardless.

The feedback we provide to users, whether diagrammatic or narrative, should be an accurate, *implementation independent* statement of the job that needs to be done. In particular, it should be as free of computerese and technical jargon as possible. A sample of diagrammatic feedback appears in Figure 2.1.

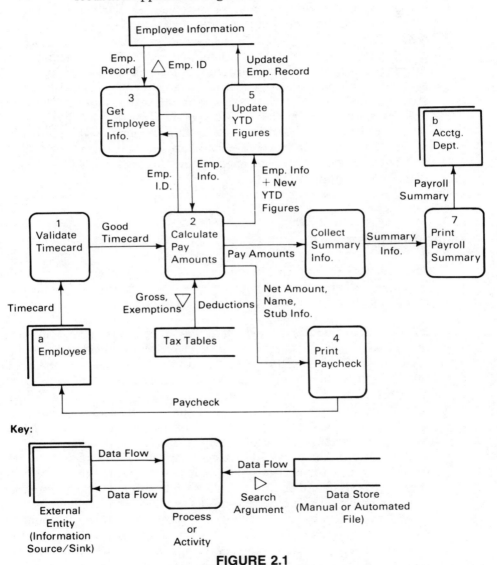

FIGURE 2.1

An Implementation Independent Description of an Information Processing Activity, in the form of a Data Flow Diagram. (See [2] and [4] in the References.)

2.2.1.2 Self-Feedback To prevent interface bugs, we also need to provide feedback to ourselves. As we begin to sketch the design of a program, presumably in the modular, hierarchical fashion described in the previous chapter, we *write down the interface assumptions.* A brief (one sentence) statement of what a calling program expects a called program to do and what information passes back and forth is exactly the kind of self-feedback we need. The statement serves as documentation, as a reference, and as a means for describing the interface in a nonprogrammed way.

Recognize that this interface statement and the actual programmed interface are two different ways of saying the same thing. A psychological fact of life is that saying the same thing in two different ways is an excellent mechanism for uncovering discrepancies and assuring that the thing is said right. Doing so at design time is the proper and constructively lazy way to go. It is effective and not much trouble, especially compared to the effort involved in finding and repairing interface bugs later.

Within a module, we write a brief statement for each major control point (loop and test). We call these statements *assertions.*

For a loop, we state (a) the conditions that should hold each time the loop scope is entered and (b) the conditions that should hold when the iteration is complete. We do *not* just write the loop test down one or two more times! We rephrase the condition in a manner that is explanatory and that helps us to check.

For example, suppose we have a loop that is to terminate when all student grade cards have been processed, and that the function of the loop is to validate the cards, separate good ones from bad ones, and maintain counts of each:

While GRADE-EOF-FLAG = 'NO'		
Grade Card (VALIDATE GRADE CARD) Test-Result		
T Test-Result = 'OK'? F		
Write Grade-Card to Good File	Write Grade-Card to Bad File	
Good-Count ← Good-Count + 1	Bad-Count ← Bad-Count + 1	
Read Next Grade-Card; on EOF, set GRADE-EOF-FLAG to 'YES'		

Assertions:

(a) Each time a loop is entered, a new grade-card should be read and ready for processing. Before the loop is entered the *first* time, Good-Count and Bad-Count should be initialized (and the first grade-card should have been read).

(b) At loop termination, all input grade-cards should be processed; each grade card should appear on either Good File or Bad File, with quantities indicated by Good-Count and Bad-Count; and Good-Count + Bad-Count should equal the original number of records.

Later, as we program, we make sure that (a) is satisfied at the point that we first enter the iteration from the outside and that it is also satisfied each time we re-enter the scope from the previous iteration. Similarly, we make sure that loop termination results in (b) being satisfied and that these assertions are appropriate for continuing on to the block of code following the loop.

For a test, we state (c) the conditions that should hold to enter each mutually exclusive block of code under control of the test (again in a slightly different phrasing than simply repeating the test), and (d) the conditions that should hold at the point that the execution paths rejoin.

During programming, we make sure that all relevant cases are handled under (c) and that no dangling possibilities are left over. Similarly, satisfying (d) means assuring that all of the parallel pathways controlled by the test create a sensible environment for execution of the code following the test.

Ultimately, we would like the ability to use these assertions (and other mechanisms) to *prove* programs correct in a mechanical and rigorous way. Some interesting research is going on in this area, but the practical ability to prove the correctness of nontrivial programs appears still to be far in the future. In the meantime, the combination of sensible assertions and a little elbow grease seems to be our best bet for doing aseptic programming—creating bug-free programs in the first place.

2.2.2   Antiseptic Programming

If some pathological organisms sneak past our aseptic barriers (and a few probably will), the next medical defense is antisepsis—steps to kill off the pathogens before they have the opportunity to do much damage. Surgical teams will paint the area of an incision with antiseptics and take other defensive measures just in case some germs get into the aseptic environment.

2.2.2.1   Defensive Programming   It makes sense to include code in our programs that makes sure events are proceeding normally and correctly and to advise us if something is wrong. By catching errors at the earliest possible moment, we reduce the distance between the occurrence of an error and its discovery, making the repair process as easy as possible.

At the same time, we do not want to go completely overboard in adding diagnostic code. These days, for example, for practical purposes, the hardware is really and truly going to work correctly all of the time. Except in rare, hardware-critical situations (e.g., nationwide telephone communications, national defense applications), there is little point in doing identical computations repeatedly to see if the answer comes out the same each time.

Remember that diagnostic code itself has at least as much likelihood of containing an error as the code being checked. Moderate amounts of diagnostic code, carefully crafted and strategically placed in a program, can greatly help to stamp out bugs. A great quantity of indiscriminate diagnostic code will get in the way and probably generate more bugs than it catches.

This says that it pays to plan ahead and to use diagnostic code judiciously. Areas for useful defensive programming include:

Echoing input data. This means printing or displaying input values immediately after they are read. We are careful, however, to display our program's *interpretation* of the input values. That is, if we read a line from a screen containing several data values, we don't just redisplay the whole line as a character string. Rather, we display the individual values, appropriately labeled, to demonstrate that the data line was divided up and stored correctly.

On the other hand, if we are processing several thousand large records, we are probably not going to echo *all* of the input. We will use the echo only initially or selectively and we may turn the echo off after we are satisfied that data interpretation is working correctly.

Eliminate dangling conditions. In a test situation, we cover all logical possibilities, including "none of the above." For example, a student status code may be "P" for part-time or "F" for full-time. Generally, it is bad practice to program:

```
If Student-Status = "P"
        Do Part-Time-Processing
Else
        Do Full-Time-Processing
```

In this program segment, bad values for Student-Code (e.g., typographical errors) will be interpreted as being equal to "F," clearly an injustice to full-time students. It is not much better to program:

```
If Student-Status = "P"
        Do Part-Time-Processing
```

```
Else
If Student-Status = "F"
    Do Full-Time-Processing
```

Now bad values just get ignored, rather than caught and reported. Appropriate defensive programming for this situation is:

```
If Student-Status = "P"
    Do Part-Time-Processing
Else
If Student-Status = "F"
    Do Full-Time-Processing
Else
    Do Bad-Student-Status-Processing
```

On the other hand, if there is a separate program or module to do data verification (that is, the bad-code case is already taken care of), there is not much point in doing the same test over and over in various other modules. In this case, simpler coding will serve.

Include control counts. Control counts check that the program has not lost any information. We count input records, for example, as we read them. We can display the count so that the person running the program can make sure we read the number of records supplied. We can compare the count with similar counts made elsewhere in processing to assure, for example, that the sum of successfully and unsuccessfully processed records equals the number we started with. Incorrect counts are a typical symptom of incorrect loop controls or a dangling condition.

Control counts also include adding up calculated percentages to make sure they sum to a reasonable approximation of 100%, and so on.

Check boundary conditions. If our program contains space for a table to be built during execution, we will certainly try to make enough space to hold all needed data. However, good defensive programming checks available space before installing the next number to make sure there is still room. "There'll never be that much data," is a classic example of Famous Last Words.

We include similar tests for magnitude of results, number of records processed (particularly if "none" has to be handled specially), etc. Some language translators build in some of these checks for us.

2.2.2.2 Walkthroughs   We obviously want to look carefully at the program development products we create. We scan our design documents and manually check our program code. We uncover some bugs this way.

However, another psychological fact of life gets in our way: We are the least likely of all observers to find flaws in our own work.

Many programmers have had the experience of unsuccessfully puzzling over a bug at great length and then going for help to a fellow programmer who finds the problem in seconds. Is the other person so much smarter than we are? Not necessarily. We can probably work the same kind of magic with other people's bugs. The point is that a person can view other people's programs more dispassionately (that is, with less ego involvement) and with fresh eyes that see what is actually on the page, not just what we *think* is there.

We can exploit this psychological magic systematically rather than using it as a last resort. In industry, programmers often work in teams, contributing to aspects of a large programming project. They will get together periodically to review each other's work in a small supportive meeting called a *structured walkthrough*.

A programmer or analyst presents one of his or her products for review. The product can be a design document, a program segment, a test data set, etc. We walk through design documents before programming begins. We walk through program code before it is computer tested (although we may remove syntax errors first and present the code as a computer listing). We similarly walk through test data and expected results before actual testing begins.

One person is designated to run the meeting and enforce the ground rules. Another takes notes. Everyone else (typically two to four others) participates by helping to look for bugs. Usual ground rules for a walkthrough are:

1. Meetings are brief to keep energy levels high.

2. Meetings are frequent so that work gets reviewed promptly.

3. Materials for review are distributed a day or so in advance.

4. No managers with hiring/firing authority are included. (In academics, no one with grading authority is included.) Participants are a peer group, which minimizes pressure.

5. Attention is exclusively directed to finding bugs, not to fixing them (for which a committee doesn't work very well) nor to discussing matters of taste or style. One useful device is to limit discussion of any topic to three minutes or less. "Works" vs. "Doesn't work" can generally be decided in this time.

6. Criticisms are directed to the product, not the producer. Questions begin "I don't understand . . ." not "Why did you . . ."

7. Any bugs found are written down in the meeting notes, for use by the product's author (see Figure 2.2). All participants sign the notes, say-

STRUCTURED WALKTHROUGH REPORT

Project: _____   Product: _____

Date: _____ / _____ / _____   Time: _____ : _____

	Signature	Name
Presenter:	_____	_____
Moderator:	_____	_____
Recorder:	_____	_____
Participant:	_____	_____
Participant:	_____	_____
Participant:	_____	_____

ACTION POINTS:

1. _____
2. _____
3. _____
4. _____
5. _____
6. _____
7. _____
8. _____

DISPOSITION: _____ Accepted   _____ Accepted with Revisions Above

_____ Major Revision and Further Walkthrough Needed

OTHER REMARKS: _____

_____

_____

_____

_____

FIGURE 2.2   Structured Walkthrough Report

ing in effect, "I have inspected this product and, except for the points noted, I accept it and take joint responsibility for its quality."

This is not as much machinery and trouble as it sounds like, and we mention walkthroughs here for a simple reason: In practice, they are the simplest and most reliable mechanism we have for assuring and promoting system quality. Classroom programming projects can be organized in this fashion as well. (See the Note on Programming Exercises in the Foreword.)

2.3 CURATIVE MEDICINE—PROGRAM DEBUGGING

In theory, by taking all of the preventive steps described above, we should end up with a program that runs correctly and completely the first time we try it. In practice, however, that is an unreasonable expectation. All of our preventives are good ones, especially (like toothpaste) when conscientiously applied. However, our preventives are also all human activities, not algorithmic or mechanical ones, and as such, slips will occur.

The preventive steps should assure that the great majority of program flaws have been weeded out in advance, just as preventive surgical medicine does avoid most postoperative infection. Some bugs may remain, however, just as postoperative infections do occasionally occur. We need a strategy to systematically wipe them out.

2.3.1 Catching Interface Bugs—Top-Down Testing

We have already observed that interface bugs are tricky because the actual error may be far removed from our evidence that something has gone wrong. Part of the problem is that in large programs there are a lot of intermodule interfaces—every big arrow on a structure chart. We can eliminate a lot of the mystery by adopting a strategy called *top-down testing* which systematically exercises and checks out the interfaces.

The main feature of top-down testing is that we don't try to test the whole program from scratch. Rather, we build a test harness that starts with only a few modules and gradually adds more, as we are satisfied that the initial modules are working cheerfully together.

As you might expect when testing is top-down, the initial modules for the test harness come from the upper part of the structure chart: the Boss module plus a few of its subordinates. In a properly constructed top-down design, the higher level modules are mainly devoted to control and coordination activities (where the interface problems are most critical) and the bulk of the actual computation is left to the lower level worker modules. We start by making sure that these high level modules are communicating properly (i.e., calling on one another at the right times and passing data appropriately). Then we add additional modules to the test harness, progressing gradually toward the lower levels of the structure chart.

The apparent problem in doing top-down testing is, how do we test a high level module without including all of the lower level modules it calls on? The answer is to include *dummy* versions of the called-on modules during early testing. We call these dummy modules *stubs*. Remember that we don't have to include stubs for all low level modules, just the ones that are called by the higher level modules in our test harness. A stub can:

- Just return without doing anything (e.g., a control count routine that we haven't implemented yet).
- Produce a trace message (i.e., display a message verifying that control arrived, and then exit).
- Produce a constant result (e.g., a coin-flipping routine that will eventually simulate this random event but which, for the moment, always returns "heads").
- Produce a rudimentary result (e.g., a tic-tac-toe move selecting routine that will eventually embody some strategy, but which for the moment just picks any unoccupied square).

Stubs themselves aren't very exciting, but remember that we are not testing the stubs, we're testing the routines that *call* on the stubs. For example, the tic-tac-toe move selector stub plays terrible tic-tac-toe, but we're not testing the strategy yet. We are trying to determine if the higher level routines call on other routines correctly, passing and accepting information in a sensible way.

As testing proceeds and results are acceptable, we selectively replace stubs by real versions of the modules and add new, even lower level stubs as needed. Eventually, we work our way down to the bottom layers of the structure chart, where no new stubs appear. Now we are testing the program in full. At each stage, including the last, we have kept careful control over the number of new interfaces that were added to the test harness. We expect, if a problem appears at some stage, that it is most likely inside, or in the interfaces to, the new modules added.

Note also that top-down testing provides an opportunity to begin program testing *early,* before all of the coding is done. If we *code* in a top-down fashion (i.e., highest level modules first), we can get the testing under way while later coding is still in progress or in prospect. In case some serious interface bugs *are* found, this interwoven programming/testing strategy can save a lot of trips down blind alleys.

2.3.2   Catching Other Bugs—Test Data and Results

To feed the top-down testing process and to catch calculation bugs as well, we need to construct sensible data on which to exercise our program. We may need to construct several versions of the test data to correspond to various stages of the top-down testing test harness. For each version, several kinds of test data are appropriate:

1. *No Data Test.* It is always instructive and useful to run a program giving it no data at all. We can't expect very exciting results, but the program should at least behave in a civilized fashion, producing a "no input data supplied" error message and terminating, or producing zero-valued results, or the like. It is not appropriate for a program to come crashing down in flames simply because no data was supplied.

2. *Good Data.* A program should be exercised most to demonstrate that it does the correct thing with good data: that calculations occur properly, that results are appropriately arrived at and displayed, etc. *Good data* typically means a series of test data sets, beginning with attempting very simple cases and working gradually toward more complex tests. The complex tests should include making the program work at the boundary of its capabilities—handling the largest numbers or greatest quantity of table entries, etc. that it is built for.

3. *Bad Data.* Finally, after we are comfortable that a program is doing what it should under favorable circumstances, we have to check its behavior under adverse circumstances. We can supply partial, incorrect, or inconsistent data to make sure that these cases are handled sensibly. One interesting test data set has values that just exceed boundary values. As in the no data case, the program should diagnose problems and behave in a civilized manner, and not shrivel up or explode.

For all test sessions, we should *predict in advance* exactly what behavior and results we expect and verify that we get them. If we have done our preventive and defensive programming thoroughly, this should happen with considerable regularity.

However, if results do not match expectations, proper debugging includes determining precisely why we got what we did. It is not sufficient merely to find an apparent error in a program. Finding one and fixing it is well and good, of course, but if the error found does not explain the observed program behavior, we have more looking to do before we run the program again.

When we *are* ready to try another run, it makes good sense to rerun all of the test data, including sets that previously worked correctly. This is our insurance that the fix we made did not disrupt a formerly working portion of the program.

2.4 CONCLUSION

For most of us, debugging is not the most attractive part of program development. It is too much a reminder of our fallibility and of the unsympathetic nature of computers where errors are concerned. This unattractiveness is the primary motivation of this chapter's emphasis on the preventive aspects of assuring program quality and correctness. Preventive debugging is generally more creative (and more fun) than curative debugging anyway.

One final time, we want to encourage you to be constructively lazy: to do the relatively easy tasks in advance that save so much trouble later on and to build programs thoughtfully in the first place, whose correctness is visible and readily verifiable.

EXERCISES

Terms You Should Know . . .

Boundary Condition   Specification Bug
Calculation Bug   Stub
Dangling Condition   Syntax Error
Defensive Programming   Top-Down Testing
Interface Bug   User Feedback
Interface Assumptions   Walkthrough
No Data Test

1. Give two examples each of specification bugs, interface bugs, and calculation bugs. Estimate, for each, the time that would be involved to find and fix the bugs.

2. Look at the program sketched in Figure 1.5 and devise a one or two sentence description of the program.

3. Take the program sketched in Figure 1.5 and annotate the control structures with assertions. Validate that the assertions hold.

4. Again, look at Figure 1.5. Suggest "good" and "bad" data sets for testing the program that would result from the sketch.

5. For each of the ground rules for a structured walkthrough, what would happen to the session if the rule was ignored or violated?

6. Explain what is demonstrated in a "no data" test of a program.

7. Explain what is demonstrated by "boundary value" tests of a program.

8. For each type of stub identified in Section 2.3.1, suggest an example other than the one given.

9. Sam coded:

```
IF A = B
     Do EQUAL-STUFF
ELSE
IF A < B
     Do LESS-STUFF
ELSE
     Do MORE-STUFF
```

Cindy argued that the default case was not being properly handled. What do you think?

10. How do each of the following structured programming concepts prevent or help to remove program bugs?

   a. Top-down design
   b. Use of black box modules
   c. Self-contained control structures
   d. Unique variable names

11. List the steps that can be taken to prevent:

   a. Interface bugs
   b. Specification bugs
   c. Calculation bugs

12. The following kinds of in-program documentation are often used to help explain how a program functions. Discuss how each kind can also prevent bugs or assist with their removal.

   a. Module description: One or two sentences at the beginning of each module describing the purpose and function of the module.
   b. Identifier catalog: A list of all variables used in the program with a brief explanation of their function.
   c. Algorithm description: A brief explanation in front of a complex calculation, data manipulation, or decision.

PART 1: REFERENCES

1. Conway, R. & Griese, D. *Primer on Structured Programming Using PL/I, PL/C, and PL/CT*. Cambridge MA: Winthrop Publishers, 1976

2. DeMarco, T. *Structured Analysis and System Specification*. Englewood Cliffs NJ: Prentice-Hall, 1979

3. Findlay, W., & Watt, D. A. *Pascal: An Introduction to Methodical Programming*. New York: Computer Science Press, 1978

4. Gane, C. & Sarson, T. *Structured Systems Analysis: Tools and techniques*. Englewood Cliffs NJ: Prentice-Hall, 1979

5. Jackson, M. *Principles of Program Design*. New York: Academic Press, 1975

6. Katzan, H., Jr. *Fortran 77*. New York: Van Nostrand Reinhold, 1978

7. Myers, G. J. *The Art of Software Testing*. New York: John Wiley & Sons, 1979

8. Nassi, I., & Shneiderman, B. "Flowcharting Techniques for Structured Programs," *ACM Sigplan Notices*. August 1973

9. Noel, P. *Structured Programming for the Cobol Programmer*. Fresno CA: Mike Murach and Associates, 1977

10. Weiland, R. J. "Experiments in Structured Cobol," *Proceedings of the CODASYL Symposium on Structured Programming in Cobol: Future and Present*. New York: ACM, Inc., 1975

11. Weiland, R. J. "Toward Understanding Algorithms," Quarterly Report No. 49, Institute for Computer Research, University of Chicago, May 1976

12. Weinberg, G. M. *The Psychology of Computer Programming*. New York: Van Nostrand Reinhold, 1971

13. Yourdon, E., Gane, C., Sarson, T., & Lister, T. *Learning to Program in Structured COBOL Part 1 and 2*. Englewood Cliffs NJ: Prentice-Hall, 1979

14. Yourdon, E., & Constantine, L. *Structured Design*. Englewood Cliffs NJ: Prentice-Hall, 1979

15. Yourdon, E. *Structured Walkthroughs* (2nd ed.). Englewood Cliffs NJ: Prentice-Hall, 1979

So, naturalists observe, a flea
Hath smaller fleas that on him prey.
And these have smaller still to bite 'em;
And so proceed ad infinitum.
Thus every poet, in his kind,
Is bit by him that comes behind.

Jonathan Swift,
"On Poetry: A Rhapsody"

2

INSIDE
THE
MACHINE

"When *I* use a word," Humpty Dumpty said, in rather a scornful tone, "it means just what I choose it to mean—neither more nor less."

"The question is," said Alice, "whether you *can* make words mean so many different things."

"The question is," said Humpty Dumpty, "which is to be master—that's all."

Lewis Carroll, *Through the Looking Glass,* Chapter 6

"It's a poor sort of memory that only works backwards."

Lewis Carroll, *Through the Looking Glass,* Chapter 5

3

BASIC COMPUTER ARCHITECTURE

In some ways, the data processing environment exists in a series of layers. At the outermost layer we have verbal, user-oriented descriptions of processes. This is succeeded by the system analyst's diagrammatic and narrative description of systems, then program and data specifications, and, finally, the programs themselves.

But computers do not even understand or operate on the programs we write in the popular programming languages, at least not directly. Computers only understand their own rather cryptic internal machine language, a layer still further in, which is generally not at all convenient for people to use. A genuine dilemma in the sensible use of computer technology is how to let people operate at the outer layers where they are comfortable, but at some distance from the inner layer where computers work.

To permit people to think like people and computers to think like computers, a series of tools can be brought to bear. We have already discussed some of these tools for system analysis, system design, and (high-level) program construction. In addition, computer technologists build translators to get from high-level programs to their computer-oriented equivalents.

While we will undoubtedly continue to spend most of our time on the people side of the division, a look at the other side is certainly useful, too. That is what Part 2 is about.

In Chapter 3, we will take a brief trip into the interior of the machine to get an idea of what's actually going on in there and what computer language programs look like.

In Chapter 4, we will take a modest look at part of the program translation process and discover along the way that programming concepts can be expressed in many ways, each appropriate for a particular purpose.

By removing a little of the mystique and mystery of The Computer, we hope to make it easier to contend with and to use as a tool.

3.1 INTRODUCTION

At the most elementary stages, it probably is not too harmful (even help-ful) to think of a computer as a code-eating, paper-generating black box. The important first concepts are those that relate to the kinds of infor-mation processing things a computer can do. However, after the initial encounters, it is helpful to discover *how* the computer works.

In this chapter, we will examine, in a general sort of way, the mech-anisms that make up a digital computer. We will not be concerned with the deeper electronics or with the details of individual information and control pathways. These are interesting and fruitful topics, but beyond the scope of our current interest. Rather, we will concentrate on the mechanisms that are immediately "visible" to and controllable by a pro-gram and programmer.

To draw an automotive analogy, we are examining the components of a car at the level of carburetor, pistons, and wheels, but not studying the underlying theory of internal combustion. Just as a functional un-derstanding of a car's insides can promote better and more efficient use of the vehicle, the objective here is to permit more intelligent and en-lightened use of a computer by delving a little into the black box.

We will look at the larger pieces that make up a computer one at a time. As necessary, we will look at the components that make up each large piece, increasing the detail at each level.

3.2 OVERVIEW—THE LARGE PIECES

A computing system is made up of considerably more equipment than the computer proper and we will make a broad distinction between the computer itself and surrounding equipment in the environment (see Fig-ure 3.1).

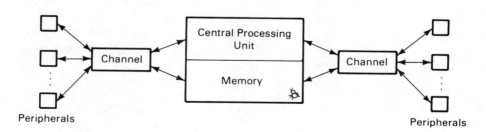

FIGURE 3.1   The Computer and Its Environment

The environment is made up of peripheral devices such as tape drives, disk drives, card readers, and printers that hold information for transmittal to and from the computer, and an additional collection of devices called *data channels* that move information back and forth between the peripherals and the computer. Peripheral devices and channels are discussed in Chapter 7.

The computer consists of a memory unit where instructions and data are stored and the central processing unit (CPU) which does the work.

3.3   MEMORY

Memory is the computer's repository for data and instructions. It is the great power of computers that a sequence of instructions can be installed into a computer to direct its behavior. We are familiar enough with computers that this fact no longer seems so remarkable, but it was the transition from hard-wired calculating machines to general purpose "stored program" computers that made modern data processing possible. And it *is* pretty remarkable that simply by loading a new program into the memory of a computer we can transform it from an accounting machine to a scientific calculator to a message switching system to a teaching machine, and on and on.

Memory is divided up into a large quantity of addressable units into which individual pieces of information can be placed. Various computers will have from several hundred to several million storage units in their memories. The size of the units will also vary from computer to computer, but there are two kinds of units that are of particular note: bytes and words.

A *byte* is enough memory space to hold one character of information and usually consists of six to nine *bits*.* Although there are some exceptions, the general tendency is for calculation oriented computers to have smallish bytes and for commercial computers (which are more text and display oriented) to have larger bytes. The larger the byte, of course, the more different characters that can be represented.

A *word* is enough space to hold a usefully large number and, in many computers, words are made up of a sequence of consecutive bytes, typically from two to eight bytes per word. For a particular computer, the word and byte size will generally be fixed. The variances are primarily from one kind of computer to another. Some computers can divide up their memories into more than one size of unit as desired, but this is less

---

*A *bit* is a "binary digit," a single 0 or 1, the basic building block of the memory of digital computers.

usual. Even in this case, the word size is usually fixed but a word can be divided into varying numbers of bytes. For example, the Univac 1100 series computers have 36-bit words that can be divided into six bytes of six bits each, or four bytes of nine bits each depending on the application running (see Figure 3.2).

Whether a computer is primarily concerned with bytes or words is reflected in the style of addressability chosen. *Addressability* means that each storage unit is associated with a unique number (its address). Programs make references to storage units by specifying their addresses. For purposes of discussion, we will concentrate on words as the storage unit.

Keep in mind that the *address* of a memory word is completely independent of the word's *contents*. For example, the word whose address is 300 may contain zero, 3.14159, −250, "ABCD", etc.

A memory word may contain a *data item* (e.g., a number to be used in a calculation or a part of a message to be printed) or an *instruction* that forms part of a program. While there is no hard and fast rule, we will often designate one portion of memory to hold data and another to hold instructions. We will take a closer look at instructions shortly.

3.4 CENTRAL PROCESSING UNIT

Among the things we want a computer to do is to take two or more items of data, combine them in a useful way to produce a useful result, and leave the result in a well-defined spot in memory. For example, we may

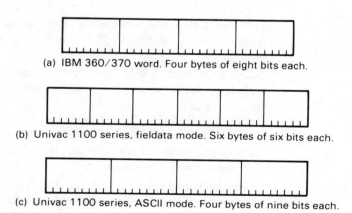

(a) IBM 360/370 word. Four bytes of eight bits each.

(b) Univac 1100 series, fieldata mode. Six bytes of six bits each.

(c) Univac 1100 series, ASCII mode. Four bytes of nine bits each.

FIGURE 3.2 Words and Bytes

want to form the sum of two numbers already in memory and place the sum in a third word. A little reflection will show that it is impractical to have direct connections from each word to every other word for making these combinations. A modest-sized memory of 25,000 storage units would require something like 300 million interconnections, and an equal number of additional interconnections would be needed for each different kind of data combination we would want to make.

3.4.1   The Arithmetic-Logic Unit

A far more economical scheme is to have a centralized area, called the arithmetic-logic unit (ALU) for doing data combination. To perform an addition, we copy the two operands from memory to spaces called *registers* in the ALU, perform the addition here, and copy the result back from the ALU to the desired memory word. This may seem more complex logistically than direct addition, but it is really a simplifying task from a design standpoint. We only need to attach enough circuitry to individual storage units to copy the units to and from the ALU registers. The circuitry for performing combinations need only operate on the registers themselves and these are typically small in number (varying from one to a couple of dozen).

In addition to these arithmetic registers (ARs), the ALU will generally contain a variety of other registers as well. Some typical ones are:

> *Adjustment register* (Adj). This register, which goes by various names in different computers, is not directly accessible to the programmer. When a calculation is performed, the data word is fetched from memory to Adj for combination with the contents of an AR. If the data word requires some adjustment prior to combination (as may be the case, for example, in floating point arithmetic), it is done in Adj.

> *Index Registers* (XRs). These are special registers that are used as counters, array subscripts, etc. In some computers, the same registers are used interchangeably as ARs and XRs. In others, XRs are separate from ARs. When separate, the XRs' size and use is often restricted and specialized. Some modest quantity of arithmetic can be done in them (usually addition and subtraction of constant amounts) and some comparisons.

> *Overflow Indicator* (OV). A one-bit register that is set to 1 if an overflow condition occurs during an arithmetic operation (i.e., an arithmetic result is too large in magnitude to fit in the result register). A program can test and reset the OV and base future execution on the value it finds.

Divide Check Indicator (DC). A one-bit register that is set to 1 when an illegal division operation is attempted (e.g., trying to divide by zero). It can be tested and reset in the same fashion as OV.

Comparison Toggle (CM). A three-way switch that is set when a program compares two values. The register is set to "less than," "equal to," or "greater than" depending on the results of the comparison. The value of CM can be tested by a program to guide execution, but the value is generally reset only by a subsequent comparison.

3.4.2   The Control Unit

Having all of these ALU registers is well and good, but how are they used? The computer operates by executing instructions and the place where instructions are noted and executed is the control unit (CU). It is the responsibility of the CU to fetch instructions from memory, decode them (determine what each instruction asks to do), and carry them out. Like the ALU, the CU has some registers into which information is placed for manipulation.

Instruction Register (IR). As with arithmetic, it is not economical to attach circuitry to each memory word for carrying out all possible instructions. Rather, instructions are fetched from memory for interpretation in the IR. Circuitry *is* attached to the IR to handle a great variety of instructions.

Instruction Location Counter (ILC). The ILC contains the memory address of the next instruction to be executed. When the CU is ready to process a new instruction, it consults the ILC to determine where the instruction is to be found. (The ILC is sometimes called the *program counter*.)

3.5   THE INSTRUCTION CYCLE

An instruction in a computer is typically composed of two major parts: (a) an operation code (opcode for short), a number or bit pattern that specifies an action to be performed, and (b) an operand that identifies a quantity that the action is done to. For example:

Opcode meaning	Operand
Add a number to AR	Memory address of the number to be added
Increase the current contents of an XR	Amount to increase it
Jump (pass control) to some specific address	The address to which control is passed

Some instructions will have more or fewer parts. Remember that while *we* will generally use a phrase or an alphabetic abbreviation to stand for an opcode, inside the computer the opcode is a string of bit values, situated in a particular portion of an instruction. (By the way, such phrases and alphabetic abbreviations are called *mnemonics,* meaning memory jogging devices.)

The cycle through which an instruction is executed is composed of three major parts:

1. *Fetch*. The instruction whose address is specified by the current contents of ILC is copied into IR.
2. *Bump*. Contents of ILC are increased by 1 (so that next time through the cycle, the next following instruction will be fetched). This new value may be altered by executing a jump instruction.
3. *Execute*. The CU interprets the contents of IR and performs the indicated activity.

The operation of this cycle is illustrated in Figure 3.3, where a set of registers and a portion of memory for a computer are shown. At the outset (Figure 3.3(a)), the ILC points to location 1000 from which the first instruction will be taken. Each remaining portion of the figure shows the state of the registers after executing one more instruction. In Figures 3.3(b) through (d), the numbers in locations 2031 and 2034 are added to the AR, and the sum in AR is compared against zero (contents of location 2000). Since the AR's contents are less than zero, CM is set to "L" and the jump in Figure 3.3(e) takes place. Note in this cycle that the ILC is reset twice: First it is bumped from 1003 to 1004 as usual. Second, the execution of the jump places the jump destination (1000) in the ILC. It is this second change that makes the jump effective, and execution resumes from location 1000.

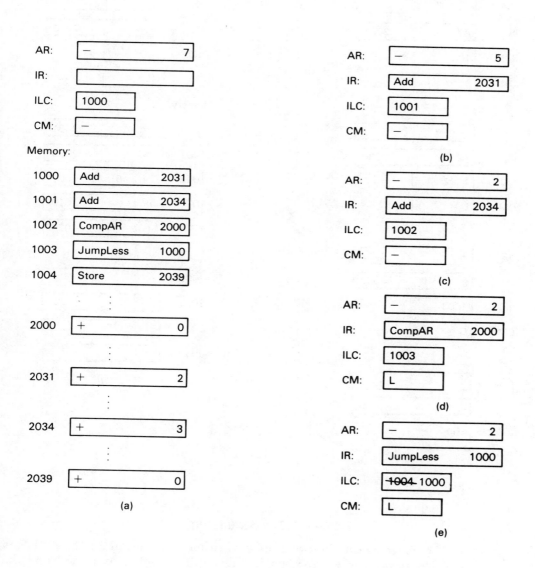

FIGURE 3.3   The Instruction Cycle

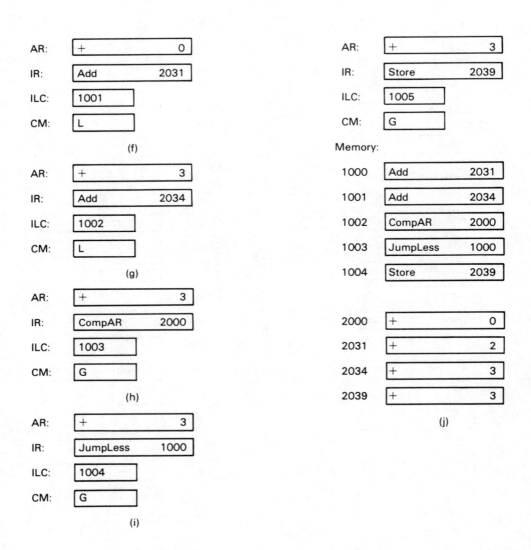

FIGURE 3.3   (Continued)

Once again, the two numbers are added to the AR and now the sum is positive. The comparison in Figure 3.3(h) sets CM to "G" and the conditional jump does not take place. Control passes to the store instruction in location 1004 which copies the AR into location 2039. The state of memory following execution of this instruction is shown at the end of Figure 3.3(j).

3.6 TERMINOLOGY

Some fairly standard terms for kinds of instruction activity have already been introduced and we hope they have been clear from context. It may be worthwhile to give some more precise definitions at this point:

Load   Copy from memory to a register. Old value of the register is lost, but the value in memory from which the load is performed is not altered.

Store   Copy from register to memory. Value of register not altered.

Compare   Determine the relation between a register and a memory location or between two registers.

Jump   Alter the sequential flow of control by changing the value in ILC. Equivalent terms are *branch* and *transfer*. Jumps may be conditional or unconditional.

Bump   Increase a register's value by 1.

3.7 STACK MACHINES

An interesting variation on the usual form of computer operation is the operation of a stack machine. In such a machine, there is a sequence of arithmetic registers that are used in a special way. Suppose these registers are given the names A[1], A[2], . . . , A[n].

At the beginning of execution, there are no particular values associated with any of the registers, and a special stack-pointer register STP contains the value zero. A load operation bumps STP and copies the contents of a memory location to A[STP].

L1: If STP = n, signal stack overflow (i.e., no more room to install information in the registers), and quit.
L2: Otherwise, set STP ← STP + 1.
L3: A[STP] ← contents of memory location to be loaded.

Conversely, a store operation first checks to see if the registers contain any useful information (i.e., STP > 0). If not, stack underflow is indicated (no information in the registers to store) and we quit. Otherwise, A[STP] is copied to memory and STP is decreased by 1.

Arithmetic is done by taking the contents of the last two occupied registers (A[STP] and A[STP − 1]), combining them as indicated by the instruction, and placing the result back into A[STP − 1]. Since we've taken out two values and put only one back, we then decrease STP by 1.

For example, in Figure 3.4, the calculation E = A*B + C*D is performed. A and B are loaded onto the stack and their product is taken (and left on the stack). C and D are loaded and *their* product is taken. Finally, the sum of these two products is formed and stored into memory cell E. We'll discuss stacks more generally in Chapter 5.

EXERCISES

Terms You Should Know . . .

Address	Instruction Cycle
Arithmetic Register	Instruction Location Counter
Arithmetic-Logic Unit	Instruction Register
Bit	Memory
Byte	Mnemonic
Central Processing Unit	Register
Control Unit	Stack Machine
Instruction	Word

1. Collating sequences: The characters used by a computer can be divided into the categories: alphabetic (A–Z), numeric (0–9), and special (everything else, e.g., $\$*\&\#.,"-+=$ and blank). Remember that each character is represented by a bit pattern that also represents a binary number. In many applications, these corresponding numbers are useful. For example, to determine that CAT comes alphabetically before DOG, we can simply look at the underlying pattern of numbers (assuming that D is represented by a larger number than C). Suggest and justify an appropriate order in which to place the characters. Should alphabetic characters come before or after numeric characters? Should they be intermixed? Where should special characters go? Is blank a special case?

2. Using Figure 3.3 as a guideline, write and trace the execution of a machine language program that calculates and prints the first five perfect squares of integers. Do this two ways, first by multiplying the appropriate integers by themselves, and second by observing that a perfect square can be obtained from the previous perfect square by adding the next odd number. That is:

$$1^2 = 1 = 0^2 + 1$$
$$2^2 = 4 = 1^2 + 3$$
$$3^2 = 9 = 2^2 + 5$$
$$4^2 = 16 = 3^2 + 7 \text{ etc.}$$

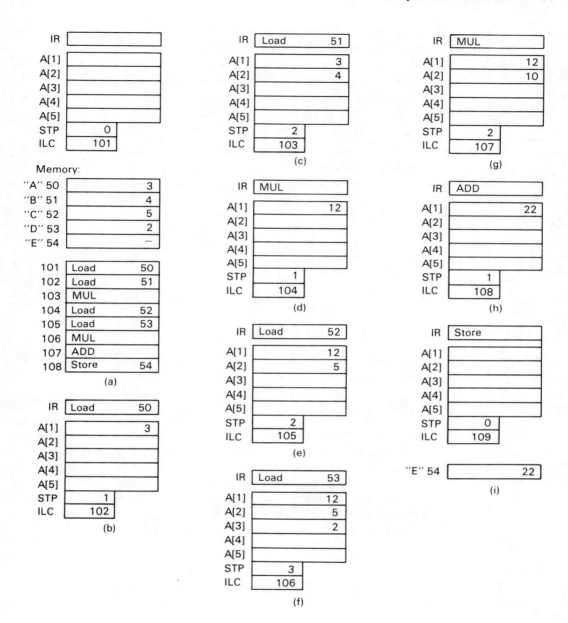

FIGURE 3.4 Stack Machine Operation

In parts (b) through (i), the state of the machine is shown *after* executing the instruction displayed in the instruction register (IR). The ILC points to the *next* instruction to be executed.

3. Using Figure 3.4 as a guideline, write and trace a stack machine program that evaluates the expression E = A ∗ (B + C) ∗ D.

4. Why is the ILC bumped *prior* to executing the instruction in the IR? For which instruction types will this make a difference?

5. How many different characters can be represented in a computer that has six-bit bytes? eight-bit bytes? nine-bit bytes? What's the generalization? What is the smallest byte size that would be practical?

6. Looking at an arbitrary word of memory, how do you know whether it contains a binary number, a string of characters, or an instruction?

7. Complete the hierarchical diagram, begun below, to describe the structure of a computer.

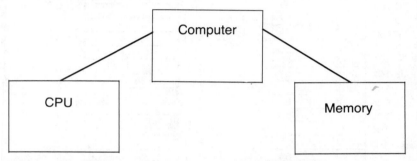

8. What is the difference between the CPU and the CU?

9. Why is it generally preferable to do arithmetic in the ALU than directly in memory?

10. Determine for the computer at your installation:
    a. Type and quantity of addressable storage units
    b. Byte size
    c. Number of arithmetic registers
    d. Number of index registers
    e. What an "Add" instruction looks like
    f. How long it takes to execute an "Add" instruction

"The cause of lightning," Alice said very decidedly, for she felt quite certain about this, "is the thunder—no, no!" she hastily corrected herself. "I meant the other way."

"It's too late to correct it," said the Red Queen: "when you've once said something, that fixes it, and you must take the consequences."

Lewis Carroll, *Through the Looking Glass,* Chapter 9

Said the Duchess: "and the moral of that is—'Be what you would seem to be'—or, if you'd like it put more simply—'Never imagine yourself not to be otherwise than what it might appear to others that what you were or might have been was not otherwise than what you had been would have appeared to them to be otherwise.' "

"I think I should understand that better," Alice said very politely, "if I had it written down."

Lewis Carroll, *Alice in Wonderland,* Chapter 9

4

WRITING AND COMPILING ARITHMETIC EXPRESSIONS

4.1 IT'S AN EXPRESSION!

In this chapter, we are going to look at several different ways of writing arithmetic expressions. We will also examine part of the process whereby a computer program gets from high-level form (e.g., Fortran, Cobol, PL/I) to machine language. One of the most interesting (although one of the trickiest) aspects of this process is translating arithmetic expressions and it is to this translation process we now direct our attention.

4.2 INFIX NOTATION

Our usual way of writing arithmetic expressions, with the operator between its operands, is called *infix*. An infix expression consists of operators, operands, and parentheses (parens, for short). We determine how an expression is to be evaluated by looking at the placement of the parens and the *precedence* of the operators. Precedence specifies which operations are to be performed first. The usual conventions are that multiplication and division have a higher precedence than addition and subtraction, so that

$$A - B/C \tag{1}$$

means that B is divided by C and *then* the quotient is subtracted from A. This arrangement can be emphasized or altered by using parens.

$$A - (B/C) \tag{2}$$

has the same meaning as [1]; the parens serve only as emphasis. However,

$$(A - B)/C \tag{3}$$

is different from [1] or [2]; it says subtract B from A and then divide the difference by C.

If we have a sequence of operators with the same precedence, they are performed left to right. The expression

$$A/B*C \tag{4}$$

means divide A by B, then multiply the quotient by C. Again, we can use parens to emphasize:

$$(A/B)*C \tag{5}$$

or alter:

A/(B*C)   [6]

Let's consider what a fairly complex arithmetic expression tells us to do:

A + B*(C/D + E)   [7]

The expression directs us to perform four separate operations:

1. Divide C by D. Call the result T_1. The expression is now $A + B*(T_1 + E)$.
2. Add T_1 and E. Call the new result T_2. The expression is now $A + B*T_2$.
3. Multiply B by T_2. Call the result T_3. The expression is now $A + T_3$.
4. Add A and T_3.

Here is another example:

Z = A*B − C*D

1. Multiply A by B. Call the result T_1.
2. Multiply C by D. Call the result T_2.
3. Subtract T_2 from T_1. Call the result T_3.
4. Store the value of T_3 into Z.

4.3   POLISH NOTATION

Another way (actually two ways) of writing arithmetic expressions was developed by the Polish logician Jan Lukasiewicz and has come to be known as Polish notation. Two features of principal interest in Polish notation are that: (a) all parentheses go away and (b) once an expression has been turned into Polish notation, we can forget about precedence— the order of operations is completely specified by the Polish expression. A third important feature of Polish notation (particularly Polish suffix), is that it is easy to translate into computer machine code. Therefore, if we can convert a normal infix expression to Polish notation, half the translation battle is over.

In our usual infix notation, we write the operator between its operands. In Polish notation, we write the operands next to each other and place the operator in front of the operands (Polish prefix) or after the operands (Polish suffix or postfix, as it is sometimes called). For example, $A + B$ in infix, becomes $+AB$ in Polish prefix, and $AB+$ in Polish suffix. More complex expressions translate in a similar fashion:

Infix	Polish Prefix	Polish Suffix	
$A + B*C$	$+A*BC$	$ABC*+$	The sum of: A and the product $B*C$
$(A + B)*C$	$*+ABC$	$AB + C*$	The product of: sum $A + B$ and C
$(A + B)*(C + D)$	$*+AB + CD$	$AB + CD + *$	A product of the two sums: $A + B$ and $C + D$
$Z = A + B$	$= Z + AB$	$ZAB + =$	The substitution of sum $A + B$ into Z

At this point we are going to leave Polish prefix alone and concentrate on Polish suffix. Let's look again at what an arithmetic expression tells us to do, this time with the expression in Polish suffix:

$ABCD/E + * +$ [8]

To analyze the expression, we scan along from left to right until we hit an operator. Then we back up and grab the two most recent operands:

1. Scanning, the first operator we hit is "/". We back up, grabbing C and D. Therefore, the first operation is: divide C by D. Call the result T_1. The expression is now $ABT_1E + * +$.
2. Continuing the scan, we hit "$+$". Back up to find T_1 and E. So add T_1 and E, and call the result T_2. The expression is now $ABT_2* +$.
3. The next operator is "$*$" and its operands are B and T_2. Multiply B by T_2, and call the result T_3. The expression is now $AT_3 +$.
4. Finally, add A and T_3.

This is, of course, exactly the same series of steps as infix expression [7], a consequence of the fact that infix $A + B*(C/D + E)$ translates to Polish suffix $ABCD/E + * +$.

Let's reason through the translation. The original expression is the sum of A and a complex expression $X_1 = B*(C/D + E)$. The Polish suffix translation will be of the form $AX_1 +$. We're not done yet, since we have still to translate the expression X_1. It is the product of B and an expression $X_2 = C/D + E$. The translation of X_1 is of the form BX_2*, and substituting into the original expression, we have advanced to $ABX_2* +$.

Similarly, X_2 translates to X_3E+ where $X_3 = C/D$ and the whole expression is now ABX_3E+*+. Finally, X_3 is the quotient C/D which translates to $CD/$, and the final form of the translation, for the whole expression is $ABCD/E+*+$.

Note that *the relative order of the operands is the same* in infix and Polish suffix; only the operators have moved.

4.4   MECHANICS OF TRANSLATING INFIX TO POLISH NOTATION

We can translate an infix expression to Polish suffix mechanically by using the algorithm shown in Figure 4.1. The basic process is to scan the infix expression from left to right. Operands, when found, are immediately transmitted to output. Operators are saved on a stack* until all of their operands have passed by. In addition, we release operators with low precedence after operators with high precedence; we release operators within parens before adjacent operators outside the parens.

For example, let's translate the input string $A-(B-C)$ to Polish suffix.

1. We start by setting our stack and output line (O) to empty and tacking a "$" to the end of the input string (I):

(empty)	I : A − (B − C) $
stack	O : (empty)

2. We get the first character "A" from the input string and begin to execute PROCESS OPERAND.

3. Since the current input character (CIC) is not "(" we bypass the initial loop of PROCESS OPERAND. Since it *is* a letter, we send it to the output line:

(empty)	I : −(B−C) $
stack	O : A

We get the next input character "−" and, since it is not ")", we skip the rest of PROCESS OPERAND and return to the main line.

---

*A *stack* is a data structure, a kind of list, in which items of data can be stored. The operation PUSH means "save an item on the stack." The operation POP means "retrieve from the stack the item most recently PUSHed that hasn't already been retrieved." We saw a stack briefly at the end of Chapter 3, and we'll discuss stacks in detail in Chapter 6.

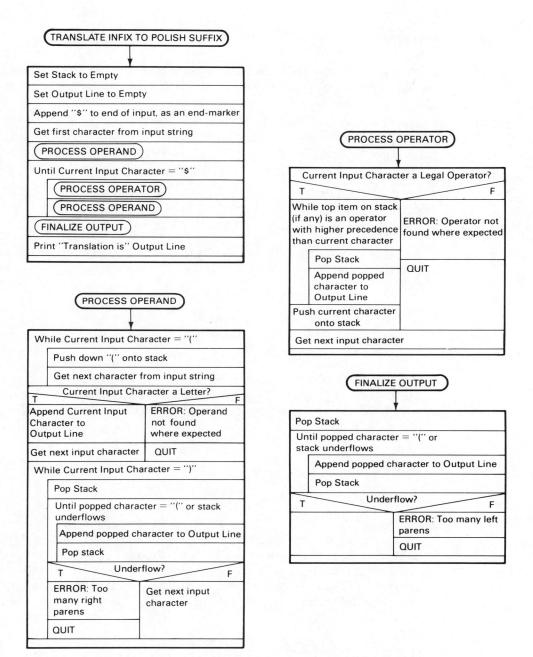

FIGURE 4.1 Infix to Polish Suffix Translation

Input to this algorithm is a sequence of characters which form an infix expression. Operators are $+,-,*,/$ with the usual precedence. Operands are single letters. Parens are allowed. Output is the Polish suffix translation of the input string or an error message (in case of error detection, a message is printed and the algorithm terminates). The algorithm uses a stack.

4. We now enter the main line's loop, which alternately executes PROCESS OPERATOR and PROCESS OPERAND until the input string is exhausted (i.e., until we encounter the "$" end marker).

5. At PROCESS OPERATOR, we find that our current input character "−" is a legal operator and, since the stack is empty, we PUSH the "−", get the next input character "(", and exit. Our status is:

$\underline{ - }$	I : B − C) $
stack	O : A
	CIC : (

6. At PROCESS OPERAND, we PUSH the "(", get the next input character "B", send it to output, get the *next* input character "−", and exit. Status is:

(	I : C) $
$\underline{ - }$	O : AB
stack	CIC : −

7. At PROCESS OPERATOR, we find that the top of the stack (i.e., the most recently pushed, not-yet-retrieved item) is not an operator, so we PUSH the "−" and get the next character "C". Status is:

−	I :) $
(	O : AB
$\underline{ - }$	CIC : C
stack	

8. At PROCESS OPERAND, we send the "C" to output, get the next input character and, since it is ")" we POP operators off the stack and send them to output, down to the matching "(". In this case, all that is sent to output is a "−". Since we stopped POPping because of a "(" rather than by emptying the stack, we get the next input character "$". Status is now:

$\underline{ - }$	I : (empty)
stack	O : ABC −
	CIC : $

9. Back in the main line, we cease iterating the main loop because the current input character is "$". We proceed to FINALIZE OUTPUT, which empties the remaining "−" off the stack, sending it to output.

Status is:

(empty)	I : (empty)
stack	O : ABC $-$ $-$

10. Finally, we arrive at the last step of the main line and print: "Translation is ABC $-$ $-$"

This may seem complicated, but in fact it is quite mechanical. You will get the hang of this algorithm quite quickly if you try a few examples yourself. (See the Exercises at the end of the chapter.)

4.5 MECHANICS OF TRANSLATING POLISH NOTATION TO MACHINE CODE

We now turn to the task of generating the instructions that correspond to an arithmetic expression via conversion of a Polish suffix string.

For demonstration purposes, we will generate instructions with the following characteristics:

1. We consider our machine to have only one arithmetic register (AR) where all arithmetic takes place, so that we don't have to worry about shuttling data between registers for different kinds of operations.

2. Our instruction set (for arithmetic expression evaluation) is:

LDA	Y	Copy the contents of memory location Y into AR (Load)
STA	Y	Copy the contents of AR into memory location Y (Store)
ADD	Y	Add the contents of memory location Y to the contents of AR (sum in AR)
SUB	Y	Subtract the contents of memory location Y from the contents of AR (difference in AR)
MUL	Y	Multiply the contents of AR by the contents of memory location Y (product in AR)
DIV	Y	Divide the contents of AR by the contents of memory location Y (quotient in AR)
COMP		Complement AR: Set the contents of AR to the negative of its previous value
INV		Invert AR: Set the contents of AR to 1 divided by the previous contents of AR

The purpose of the last two instructions is to handle a problem in the use of stacks: that it turns the order of the operands around. The code corresponding to the Polish string AB − (equivalent to infix A − B) will turn out to be:

```
LDA    B
SUB    A
COMP
```

A more sophisticated translator than the one we are describing can turn out simpler code, but the algorithm is considerably more complicated than the one shown. Alternatively, we could make a post-translation pass across the generated code to simplify it. This process is left as an exercise.

Our process for generating code from a Polish suffix string pretty much follows the rules given previously: we scan along the string until we find an operator then back up, creating an operation that uses the previous two operands. In many cases, one of the operands will be the result of the last operation. In this case, that operand will (at execution time) already be waiting in AR and one instruction is generated to combine it with the other operand (to leave a new result in AR). In other cases, two instructions must be generated: one to load the first operand into AR, the other to perform the operation that combines the second operand with the first. We will use a variable OP-FLAG in the algorithms to keep track of which case applies. The algorithm is shown in Figure 4.2.

As a simple example, let's see what the algorithm does with ABC − D/ = which is equivalent to A = (B − C)/D.

1. We set our stack to empty, we zero OP-FLAG and TEMP-COUNT, get the first character from the input string "A", and enter the main loop. Our status is:

$$I : B\ C\ -\ D/ =$$

(empty)	CIC : A
stack	OP-FLAG : 0
	TEMP-COUNT : 0

2. Since we have a letter, we enter PROCESS OPERAND where we simply PUSH the "A" and return.

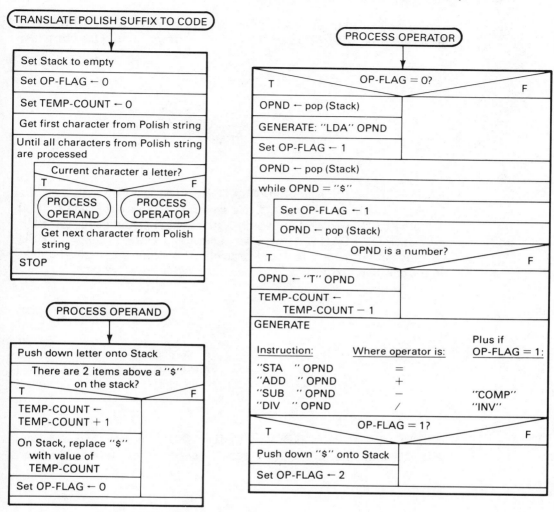

FIGURE 4.2   Polish Suffix to Code Translation

Input to the algorithm is a (correct) Polish suffix string. The output is a sequence of instructions that corresponds to the string. The algorithm uses a stack which has the special feature that we can get at items in the middle if we need to. The stack holds operands until they are needed. The special marker "$" is placed on the list to indicate an operand is the result of a previous calculation and resides in AR. Operands that are temporary storage items (of the form T1, T2, etc.) are indicated on the stack by digits. The running count of temporary variables is maintained in TEMP-COUNT. The OP-FLAG variable provides information on the state of the calculation. OP-FLAG = 0 means AR will be unoccupied at this point of the evaluation at execution time. OP-FLAG = 1 means that AR will contain the right operand of the next calculation; OP-FLAG = 2 means the left operand. Keep in mind, in reading the algorithm, that several of the algorithm variables contain alphabetic information. Thus if X contains "3", the substitution Y ← "T" X results in Y receiving the value "T3".

3. Our main loop gets "B", calls PROCESS OPERAND to PUSH the "B", does the same with "C", and then gets "−" from input. Our status is:

C		I : D/ =
B		CIC : −
A	output	OP-FLAG : 0
stack	(empty)	TEMP-COUNT : 0

4. Now we enter PROCESS OPERATOR. Since OP-FLAG is zero, we POP the stack, retrieving "C". We generate the output "LDA C" and set OP-FLAG to 1. We POP again, retrieving "B", and generate "SUB B". Since OP-FLAG is 1, we also generate "COMP"; then we PUSH "$" and set OP-FLAG to 2 and return to the main line to get the next input character. Status is:

$		
A	output	I : / =
stack	LDA C	CIC : D
	SUB B	OP-FLAG : 2
	COMP	TEMP-COUNT : 0

5. At PROCESS OPERAND, we PUSH the "D". There is now one item above a $ on the stack. We return to get the next input character. Status is:

D		
$		I : =
A	output	CIC : /
stack	LDA C	OP-FLAG : 2
	SUB B	TEMP-COUNT : 0
	COMP	

6. At PROCESS OPERATOR, we generate "DIV D" (but no "INV" since OP-FLAG ≠ 1). We return to get the next input character. Status is:

```
    $                                              | : (empty)
    A                  output                     CIC : =
  ―――――                ―――――――                 OP-FLAG : 2
  stack              LDA   C              TEMP-COUNT : 0
                     SUB   B
                     COMP
                     DIV   D
```

7. Again at PROCESS OPERATOR, we POP the "$" which resets OP-FLAG to 1, and generate "STA A". Having exhausted the input string, we quit. The output has been:

```
LDA   C
SUB   B
COMP
DIV   D
STA   A
```

the instructions corresponding to our arithmetic expression.

There is one other problem we need to handle in compiling code, illustrated by the following arithmetic expression:

$$(A+B)*(C+D) \text{ or } AB+CD+*$$

To evaluate this expression, we must form two sums $(A+B$ and $C+D)$ and then multiply the two sums together. We will need the use of AR for forming each sum. Consequently, after forming $A+B$ we will have to save this result in a memory location, leaving AR free to calculate the other sum. When $B+C$ has been formed in AR, we multiply it by the saved value. The complete code might be:

```
LDA   B
ADD   A     Sum A + B is in AR
STA   T1    Save sum in a temporary storage location
LDA   D
ADD   C     Sum C + D is in AR
MUL   T1    Multiply by saved value
```

Try working this through the algorithm. Remember in looking at the algorithm that it specifies a translation process. To do translations correctly, it must anticipate what the generated instructions will do during execution, but the algorithm does not itself evaluate the arithmetic expression.

Now that we know how to translate from infix to Polish suffix and from Polish suffix to code, we know how to go from infix to code, simply by applying the two algorithms one after another. If there is an error in the arithmetic expression, the first algorithm will catch it and the second algorithm will be bypassed. If the infix expression is a correct one, we translate it to code in the two stages described.

It is also possible to write a single algorithm that translates directly from infix to code without going through the intermediary of Polish suffix. Such an algorithm is a fairly natural combination of features of the two algorithms we have seen, using two stacks: one for operators, like Figure 4.1, and one for operands, like Figure 4.2. The details of this combined algorithm are left as an exercise.

EXERCISES

Terms You Should Know . . .

Infix	Polish Prefix
Operand	Polish Suffix
Operator	Precedence

Basic Skills

1. Translate the following infix expressions to Polish prefix and to Polish suffix:

    i. $A*B + C$ vi. $A + B - C + D$
    ii. $(A*B) + C$ vii. $Z = P/(Q - R)$
    iii. $A*(B + C)$ viii. $W = R/S + T - U$
    iv. $A*B - C/D$ ix. $A = T - (U - V*W)$
    v. $A + (B + (C + D))$ x. $A = T - ((U - V)*W)$

2. For the infix expressions shown in parts (ix) and (x) of Problem 1, describe the sequence of operations that are to be carried out.

3. Translate the following Polish suffix expressions to infix:

    i. $ABD + /FG - K* -$
    ii. $GHJKLMP + - + - + =$
    iii. $GHJ + K - L + MP - + =$
    iv. $PDQ//$
    v. $APDQ//GHI - - + =$

4. For the Polish suffix expression described in part (v) of Problem 3, describe the sequence of operations that is to be carried out.

5. Using the algorithm shown in Figure 4.2, translate each of the Polish suffix expressions from Problem 3 into machine code.

6. Why is "precedence" a meaningful concept for infix expressions but not for Polish suffix expressions?

Intermediate Problems and Extended Concepts

7. Devise an algorithm that examines a stream of generated machine instructions and rearranges code, where appropriate, to eliminate INV and COMP instructions.

8. Define two new instructions called RSUB and RDIV:

   RSUB Y   Subtracts the contents of AR from the contents of memory location Y, leaving the difference in AR (value of Y unchanged)

   RDIV Y   Divide the contents of memory location Y by the contents of AR, leaving the quotient in AR (Y unchanged)

   Revise the algorithm of Figure 4.2 to use these two new instructions and eliminate the use of INV and COMP.

9. Using the hints provided in the text, devise an algorithm that translates directly from infix to code without going through Polish suffix as an intermediary.

10. Devise an algorithm to translate between Polish prefix notation and Polish suffix notation. (Hints: Note that Polish prefix and Polish suffix are not merely reversals of one another. For one thing, operands will appear in the *same* order in each. Also, not that infix A*(B + C) is *A + BC in Polish prefix but ABC + * in Polish suffix. You may find that a recursive approach is helpful here.)

11. Devise a simple set of rules for scanning a character string left-to-right and determining whether it is a legal Polish suffix expression. Assume operands are single letters and operators are +, −, *, /. (Note that AB + + is *not* legal; it has too many operators. Similarly, ABC + has too few. AB + + C has operators misplaced.)

PART 2: REFERENCES

1. Aho, A. V., & Ullman, J. D. *The Theory of Parsing, Translation, and Compiling.* Englewood Cliffs NJ: Prentice-Hall, 1972

2. Floyd, R. W. "Syntactic Analysis and Operator Precedence," *Journal of the ACM,* 10(3), 1963

3. Foster, C. C. *Computer Architecture.* New York: Van Nostrand Reinhold, 1970

4. Glass, R. L. "An Elementary Discussion of Compiler/Interpreter Writing," *ACM Computing Surveys,* 1(1), March 1969

5. Gries, D. *Compiler Construction for Digital Computers.* New York: John Wiley & Sons, 1971

6. Reddi, S. S., & Feustel, E. A. "A Conceptual Framework for Computer Architecture," *ACM Computing Surveys,* 8(2), June 1976

In the popular conception, a computer is a high-speed number calculator. This view is only partly correct. A digital computer is, in fact, a general symbol-processing device, capable of performing any well-defined process for the manipulation and transformation of information.

Edward Feigenbaum and Julian
Feldman, *Computers and Thought*

High speed stores contain typically millions of bits. . . . If we dare to attach a meaning to such a vast amount of bits, we can only do so by grouping them in such a way that we can distinguish some sort of structure in the vast amount of information. . . . The structure is *our* invention and *not* an inherent property of the equipment.

E. W. Dijkstra, *Acta Informatica I*
(1971)

3

NONNUMERIC METHODS

The world of data processing is divided roughly into two parts. The first is formally called scientific data processing. Into this field fall most of the areas that the layman and neophyte generally associate with computers—statistical analysis, molecular wave vibration computations, the calculation of pi to three million decimal places, numeric solutions of differential equations, determining whether that rocket is actually going to make it to the moon, and so on.

When the speed of a computer is discussed, the criterion is often how many "adds" per second the machine can perform. The newcomer to computer science is most often exposed, initially and primarily, to this aspect of data processing. The computer languages that are taught and the programs that are assigned are nearly always oriented in this direction. But . . .

Underlying much of the work in the scientific area, and comprising an area itself at least as large, are nonnumeric methods. The area is so called, not because it does without numbers (it doesn't), and not because we never perform a multiplication (occasionally we will), but rather because arithmetic processing per se is simply incidental or peripheral to the study. The representation of information, the design and management of files, text processing and analysis, and the manipulation of data structures are all classed in this area.

In Part 3 we are going to look at three aspects of nonnumeric methods: data structures, searching and sorting, and file management. Each of these topics is the subject of whole books and, in this brief treatment, you are obviously not going to find out All There Is To Know about nonnumeric methods. What we will try to achieve in the next three chapters is the communication of particularly prominent and useful techniques and facts, and more important, the flavor of nonnumeric work and an appreciation for the vast field of study beyond numeric methods.

'O Oysters, come and walk with us!
  The Walrus did beseech.
'A pleasant walk, a pleasant talk,
  Along the briny beach:
We cannot do with more than four,
  To give a hand to each.' . . .

Four young Oysters hurried up,
  All eager for the treat:
Their coats were brushed, their faces washed,
  Their shoes were clean and neat—
And this was odd, because, you know,
  They hadn't any feet.

Four other Oysters followed them,
  And yet another four;
And thick and fast they came at last,
  And more, and more, and more
All hopping through the frothy waves,
  And scrambling to the shore.

Lewis Carroll, *Through the
Looking Glass*, Chapter 4

"I'm very glad," said Pooh happily, "that I thought of
giving you a Useful Pot to put things in."

"I'm very glad," said Piglet happily, "that I thought of
giving you Something to put in a Useful Pot."

A. A. Milne, *Winnie-The-Pooh*

5

DATA STRUCTURES

5.1 "IN THE BEGINNING WAS THE WORD"

The first thing to get clear in our minds is the difference between a data structure and a storage structure. You already know the difference between an algorithm, which is the abstract specification of a process; a computer program, which is the mapping of the algorithm into a particular computer language; and an object program, which is the translation of the computer language into an internal representation of bits and bytes that resides within and can be executed by the computer.

Similarly, we must keep in mind the distinction between a data structure in the abstract (an array, tree, list, queue, stack) and the representation of this structure on a storage device. In addition and distinct from both of these is the set of values that may occupy a structure at any particular moment in time. Abstractly, we may think of a rectangular matrix as an empty chessboard, or as an array of elements:

$$
\begin{array}{cccc}
A_{11} & A_{12} & \cdots & A_{1n} \\
A_{21} & A_{22} & \cdots & A_{2n} \\
\cdot & & & \cdot \\
\cdot & \cdots & & \cdot \\
\cdot & & & \cdot \\
A_{m1} & A_{m2} & & A_{mn}
\end{array}
$$

In the memory of a computer, this matrix needs $n \times m$ memory slots along with the information that maps a pair of subscripts to a particular slot. These slots *might* all contain zero; slot A_{ij} *might* contain $\log(2i)\sin(j)$; there may be no value in particular associated with the slots.

The nice, straightforward linear or multidimensional array is the first nontrivial data structure encountered by a new programmer, and it is often the source of some initial headaches. At this point in your careers, however, this form of data structure should be sufficiently familiar that we can begin to play some tricks with it.

5.2 TABLES

5.2.1 Basic Notions

The first extension of the simple array is the *table*. Consider the price schedule depicted in Figure 5.1. We can represent this table in almost any computer language as a two-dimensional array. The columns of the array are listings of different kinds of information (quantity, base cost, etc.) while each row represents an aggregate of all the information for a

Quantity	Amount	Plus Extras @
0	0	60
10	600	50
50	2600	40
100	4600	30
200	7600	25
.	.	.
.	.	.

FIGURE 5.1

A price table, representable as an N×3 array. If the quantity ordered is between PRICE [k,1] and PRICE [k+1,1], then the cost is PRICE [k,2] plus (quantity ordered− PRICE [k,1]) * PRICE [k,3].

particular case. The first subscript of the array selects a row, the second a column.

It is possible to use a single array for this example since all the information is of one type (integer). Figure 5.2 illustrates an example where, in many programming languages, this is not so. Part of the information contained in this table is integral, part real, and part character. A separate array will often be needed for each data element, although only one table is being stored. Note, however, that a single index gives us access to an entire row of the table. Part number 029 is in the sixth row of the table: the part number is stored in PARTNO[6]. Similarly, the part name is in the sixth row of the PNAME array and the unit price is in PRICE[6].

Part No.	Part Name	Unit Price
001	Left-handed blivet	.28
002	Right-handed blivet	.28
003	Ambidextrous blivet	.42
005	Pressure bonds	2.50
007	j-bonds	6.75
029	Key punch	945.00
030	Off-key punch	2.25
031	Nice Hawaiian punch	.39
.	.	.
.	.	.

FIGURE 5.2

Another kind of price table, represented as several arrays. Row k of the table is represented by the items PARTNO [k] and PRICE [k] and the kth row of array PNAME.

Using a separate array for each element also has the pleasant advantage of introducing a meaningful name for each kind of data. We will often want to make use of this naming ability even when we could have used a single multi-dimensional array.

5.2.2   The Value as an Index

In all of the above, we assumed that the table was packed. The term *packed* here does not mean completely filled; it means that there are no gaps in the table. If the table size was 100 rows and there were 25 items in it, we expect these items to occupy the first 25 slots and the remaining 75 to be "empty." This doesn't have to be the case.

Suppose that the part numbers were all in the range 1 to 100. We could then store the price of item 029 in PRICE[29], the name of the item in row 29 of PNAME, and eliminate the PARTNO array altogether. This scheme makes looking up a name and price very much faster. Instead of having to look through the PARTNO array to discover which subscript to use for accessing the other arrays, we can use the part number itself as the index and access the related information directly. There may now be gaps in our arrays: given the table of Figure 5.2, PRICE[4], PRICE[6], etc. would contain no useful information although a special value (such as -1) might be stored in them to indicate that they are empty. In some respects this is useful. In the original packed scheme, if we suddenly acquired a part whose number was 4, we would have had to move all items with part numbers larger than 4 down a notch to make room for the new entry. In the unpacked scheme, we simply drop the relevant information into the fourth position of each array where room is already available.

This value-as-index scheme is useful and practicable where the set of values an entity can take on is reasonably small, and where the percentage of the values that actually occur is reasonably large. What "reasonably" means depends on the availability of space (how much can be wasted as gaps) and the premium placed on speed.

All of this illustrates two basic points that constantly recur in all data processing work: (a) it pays to think about the variety of information you are dealing with before charging ahead and (b) there is always a trade-off. A *trade-off* means you can expend one commodity to conserve another. Programs typically can be sped up if they are allowed to occupy more space; space can be saved by using a slower procedure (we could after all, have eliminated those extra 75 rows in the packed scheme); a program will run faster *and* in less space if great care is taken in its writing; a program can be gotten off the drawing board and into production more rapidly if we're willing to sacrifice a certain amount of efficiency. We will see numerous examples of trade-offs throughout this section.

5.2.3 Hashing

It will sometimes happen that the conditions for using the value-as-index scheme are exactly wrong—the range of possible values is very large and the number of values actually used is very small. An example of this is the building of a symbol table by a compiler or assembler. In most programming languages, you can choose variable names from among millions of possibilities, but it is a rare program that uses as many as a hundred or two of these possible values. Yet, the compiler must keep track of each symbol you use, plus a considerable amount of related information (data type, whether an array, etc., etc.). Since the compiler itself is a large program, it cannot afford to waste much space. Since it is used frequently, it must be quick. There is a technique that can be used under these constraints which transforms the symbol itself into an index to a storage table. This process is called *hashing*. Consider the following example:

Suppose we allow a table size of 512 ($= 2^9$). We take the bits that actually compose the name we wish to store and perform some series of manipulations on them. We take nine bits from the middle of the result to give us a number in the range 0–511 to use as an index. We then store all of the information related to this name (including the name itself) in the selected table row. Figure 5.3 illustrates an example of this method which requires only about five machine language instructions to give us an index. Note in Figure 5.3 that two very similar symbols (RMF and RNF) produce very different index values. This is a desirable characteristic since similar symbols are common in many programs and we would like to avoid having symbols bunch up in one part of the table.

No matter how good the hashing function is, however, occasionally there will be a collision; that is, the function returns the same index value for two different symbols. When the table slot indicated by the index is already occupied, we can either search down the table from the given index until an empty slot is found or perform *another* hash on the middle 15 bits of the result of the first hash using the same or a different hashing function. Although this scheme requires some careful programming, it is quick and saves space. Figure 5.4 shows that filling a table 90% full requires, on the average, only about 2.5 tries to find a slot for each symbol. This same figure is the average number of tries we have to make to *find* a symbol in the table.

When we want to get information on a name out of the table, we rehash the name to give us the table index. We always check the actual name stored there to make sure that we've found the information we want. If it doesn't match, we assume a collision occurred when our information was stored, and use the mechanism that was used to store colliding data. (How do we discover that the information we seek is not in the table at all?)

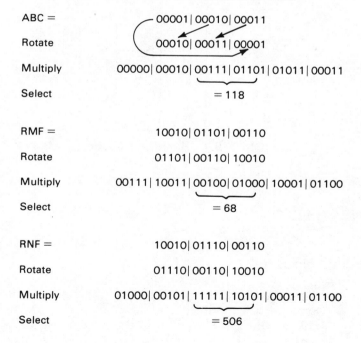

A Hashing Scheme

Represent the letters of the alphabet by the five-digit binary numbers from 1 to 26 (A = 00001, B = 00010, . . . Z = 11010). Let the symbols be three letters long. Let our table have 512 rows. The hashing function is:

1. Rotate the symbol left five bits.

2. Multiply the result of (1) by the original symbol. Pad with leading zeros to make the product 30 bits long.

3. Select bits 11–19 of the product. These represent a number from 0 to 511. Use this number as the index to the table.

ABC =   00001| 00010| 00011

Rotate   00010| 00011| 00001

Multiply   00000| 00010| 00111| 01101| 01011| 00011

Select   = 118

RMF =   10010| 01101| 00110

Rotate   01101| 00110| 10010

Multiply   00111| 10011| 00100| 01000| 10001| 01100

Select   = 68

RNF =   10010| 01110| 00110

Rotate   01110| 00110| 10010

Multiply   01000| 00101| 11111| 10101| 00011| 01100

Select   = 506

FIGURE 5.3 Hashing

When the table is a fraction f full, the expected number of tries we have to make to find an empty table slot for a new entry is:

$$E(f) = (1 - f) + 2(1 - f)f + 3(1 - f)f^2 + \ldots$$
$$= 1 - f + 2f - 2f^2 + 3f^2 - \ldots$$
$$= 1 + f + f^2 + \ldots$$
$$= \frac{1}{(1 - f)}$$

However, the *average* number of tries we have to make to fill an empty table of size N (N fairly large) to a fraction f is approximated by:

$$\bar{E}(f) = \frac{1}{Nf} \int_0^{Nf} \frac{1}{1 - \dfrac{n}{N}}\, dn$$

Substituting $t = 1 - \dfrac{n}{N}$ we get

$$\bar{E}(f) = -\frac{1}{f} \int_1^{1-f} \frac{1}{t}\, dt = -\frac{1}{f} \ln(1 - f)$$

f	E(f)	$\bar{E}(f)$
.1	1.11	1.05
.5	2.	1.39
.75	4.	1.85
.9	10.	2.56

FIGURE 5.4   Hashing Function Statistics

5.3   LINEAR LISTS

5.3.1   Basic Notions

After the array, the next simplest information structure is the linear list. Such a list is a collection of nodes (slots into which data can be put), each one of which is connected to the next. Most nodes in the list will have both a predecessor and a successor. There are also two special cases, the "first" node, which has no predecessor, and the "last" node, which has no successor. A special case of a list is the *null list,* which contains no nodes.

5.3.2   Stacks and Queues

Certain linear lists are given special names, which are not based on the structure of the list, but on the operations that may be performed on them.

If a linear list may have nodes added and deleted only at *one end* of the list, it is called a *stack*. The classic example of a stack is the pile of trays in a cafeteria. As trays are added to the top of the pile, springs under the pile compress so that the top of the pile remains at about the same level. When we take a tray off the top, the next one rises to the top position. For reasons no better than this, the operation of adding a node to a stack is called *pushing down* and the removal of a node is called *popping up*. Stacks are also called push down lists (PDLs) or LIFO (Last In, First Out) lists. Stacks are used in innumerable computer applications, particularly in recursive processes, translations, and multiprogramming.

A linear list in which additions to the list are made at one end and removals at the other is called a *queue* or FIFO (First In, First Out) list. The checkout line at the grocery store and any pipeline are examples of queues.

5.3.3   Internal Representation

Sequential Allocation   Stacks and queues can be represented in memory as a contiguous block. For convenience, we assume that each node is one word long. Let us suppose we have set aside a block of memory called LIST that is L words long.

For the representation of a stack we need one additional word, the stack pointer (STP) to tell us where the top of the stack is at the moment. We initialize STP to zero. This means that the stack is initially empty, or null. Now, unlike the cafeteria tray example, we do not actually shove information one notch further down each time we add a new entry. This is far too cumbersome. Rather, we operate as follows:

To add an item to the stack, we first add 1 to STP and then store the item in LIST[STP]. Conversely, to remove an item, we retrieve LIST[STP] and then subtract 1 from STP. If we try to make STP larger than L, an error return must be given since there is no more space in LIST to store items. Similarly, a request to remove an item from the stack when STP is zero (i.e., when the stack is empty) is also an error.

The representation of queues is slightly more complicated. We need two pointers, one for each end of the list. Call these F and R for front and rear. (We add items at the rear and remove them from the front, just like a waiting line.) We initialize both F and R to 1. To add an item to the queue, we first increment R and then store the item in LIST[R]. To remove an item, we increment F and then retrieve LIST[F].

Because LIST is finite, we cannot let R and F increase indefinitely. Observe that as F is incremented, all of the list items LIST[k] with k<F are available for reuse. Therefore, when R (or F) gets to be as large as L (pointing to the end of the list), on the next increment we set it back to 1. In this fashion F chases R round and round the list.

Error conditions arise if F catches up with and tries to pass R (attempt to remove nonstored item) or if R gets so large that it catches up with F (attempt to put more than L − 1 items into the queue. Why only L − 1?).

Linked Lists   The major difficulty in using contiguous blocks of memory for the storage of lists is that additions and deletions at the middle of the list are awkward and we must put a fixed bound on the size of the list. If we have only one list, we can always allocate all of available storage to it, but this is wasteful since we may only be using a small portion of this memory at any one time. If we have several lists, we must assign some bound to each. However, there is another way to parcel out memory that allows much greater flexibility.

In this scheme, each node within a list contains, in addition to the data item stored, the address (or subscript) of the next item on the list. Each node can be stored in an arbitrary location in memory. However, if we keep a record of where the first node is, all others can be found by tracing along these pointers: the first node tells us where the second node is, the second where the third node is, and so on. (Compare Figures 5.5(a) and 5.5(b).) In the sequential scheme, we maintained indexes independent of the list to tell us where in the list we were looking. For a linked list, we keep pointers to memory cells which contain the addresses of the nodes under consideration.

Certain list operations are made far easier in the linked scheme. These include adding a node anywhere on the list, deleting a node, and

Address	Name		
1043	LIST [1]	+	253
1044	LIST [2]	−	16
1045	LIST [3]	+	0
1046	LIST [4]	+	37
1047	LIST [5]	+	172
1048	LIST [6]	−	3

FIGURE 5.5(a)   A List Stored Sequentially in Memory.

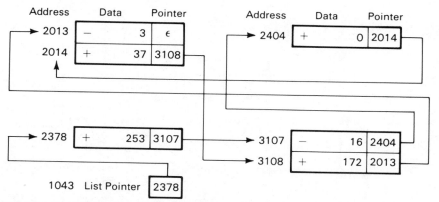

FIGURE 5.5(b)   A List Stored Arbitrarily in Memory, with Connecting Links.

The symbol "ε" stands for the null link or null pointer and signifies the end of the list. If the pointer field of location 2013 contained 2378 instead of ε, the list would be circular.

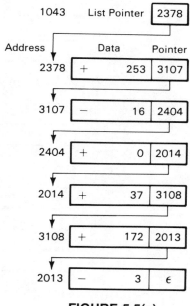

FIGURE 5.5(c)

The same linked list as Figure 5.5(b), but with the nodes appearing in order of appearance in the list, rather than by memory location.

Address	Name		
1043	LIST [1]	+	253
1044	LIST [2]	−	16
1045	LIST [3]	+	37
1046	LIST [4]	+	172
1047	LIST [5]	−	3
1048	LIST [6]	· · ·	

FIGURE 5.5(d)

The same sequential list as Figure 5.5(a), but with the third item of that list deleted, and all the remaining items moved up one notch.

concatenating several lists. To delete node k, for example, we simply make node k − 1 point to node k + 1. In the sequential scheme, we would have had to move all nodes beyond node k up one notch to fill the gap left by deleting node k.

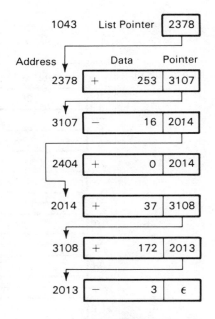

FIGURE 5.5(e)

The same linked list as Figure 5.5(b) and 5.5(c), but with the third node deleted. Note that the node at 2404 is out of the list simply because it is not pointed to, either by the list pointer or another list node.

On the other hand, operations such as finding the jth node are much slower in a linked list. In the sequential list, we could merely have accessed LIST [j]. In the linked scheme, we must start at the first node and follow the pointers till we arrive at node j. Also, depending on how much of a memory location is taken up by the data item, the linked list may require more space for each node, since a pointer must also be stored. (When will a node of a linked list occupy no more space than in a sequentially stored list?)

The *allocation* of storage, however, can be far more efficient. We can maintain a pool of available storage words, all linked together. When any of our lists needs to expand, it can draw a word from this pool. Similarly, when a word is no longer needed by the list, it can return the word (i.e., relink it) to the pool. Schemes of this kind are called *dynamic allocators*. (What kind of structure would be most efficient for the pool of available words?)

Recall that when we represented a queue using sequential storage and one of our indexes reached the end of the list, we reset the index to point to the first element. The dynamic allocation of storage for a linked list makes this kind of recycling unnecessary—the list will contain exactly the number of words it currently needs, no more, no less.

There are occasions, however, when it pays to maintain a linked list of a fixed size and to do without dynamic allocation (for example, when we *know* that a list will never need to be more than n nodes long, and that most of the time its size will not be much less than n). In such cases, we would like our pointers to be able to get conveniently from the last node of the list back to the first. An easy way to accomplish this is to link the last node to the first. This, in effect, completes a circle of nodes, each one pointing to the next. Such a structure is called a *circular* list.

A simple generalization of the linked list is the *double linked list,* where each node contains a pointer both to its successor (as before) *and* to its predecessor. In a *double linked circular list,* not only does the last node point back to the first, but vice-versa also. (See Figure 5.6. What are the advantages and disadvantages of double linking?)

5.4   TREES

5.4.1   Graphs

Graph theory is a field quite as extensive as set theory. For the purpose at hand, however, we simply require a few definitions. First of all, we are *not* talking about the kinds of graphs that are drawn on graph paper, showing the functional relationship between two variables. In this section, graphs are collections of interconnected objects called nodes. (See

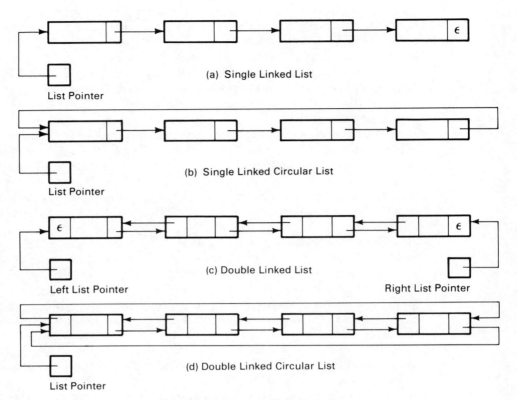

FIGURE 5.6   Linked Lists

Figure 5.7(a).) In speaking of graphs, we will consider only graphs with a finite number of nodes.

1. A graph G is a set of nodes N = $\{x_1, x_2, \ldots x_n\}$, and a set of *pairs* of nodes called *arcs,* where each element of each pair is in N.
2. Two nodes x_i and x_j are said to be *adjacent* if there is an arc joining them.
3. Given a sequence of nodes, each adjacent to the next, the sequence of arcs joining the nodes is called a *path.*
4. Two nodes are said to be *connected* if there is a path between them.
5. If all pairs of nodes in the graph are connected, then the graph is said to be connected.
6. If a node is connected to itself, the path from the node to itself is called a *loop.*

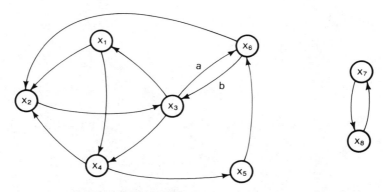

FIGURE 5.7(a)   A Typical Graph

Nodes are $x_1, \ldots, x_8$. The arcs are represented by the arrows that join the nodes. Note that there are *two* arcs joining x_3 and x_6, one going each way. We can distinguish the arcs by labeling them, as in the figure, or by writing an ordered pair: Arc a can also be written (x_3,x_6). Arc b can be written (x_6,x_3). The order is (tail,head). One loop in this graph is (x_3,x_4,x_5,x_6).

5.4.2   Properties of Trees

A *tree* is a nonempty, connected, loop-free graph with one particular node identified as the *root*. In a diagram of a tree, the root (unlike in nature) conventionally appears at the top and all other nodes descend from it. Speaking of descent, the standard terminology calls nodes adjacent to the root the root's *sons* (or daughters or children). They are themselves *siblings* and the root is their *father* (or mother or parent). Other terminology is analogous.

If we remove the root and its associated arcs from the tree, we will have left a set of subtrees (unless the original tree contained only the root, in which case its removal leaves nothing at all). Each of these subtrees is itself a tree whose root is a son of the original root. A node that has no descendants is called *terminal*. (See Figure 5.7(b).)

Among the many areas in computer science where trees play an important role is the study of natural and formal languages and, in particular, the construction and parsing of arithmetic expressions. Figure 5.8 shows how a tree may be used to resolve the ambiguity in the sentence, "The boy hit the man with the apple." Figure 5.9 illustrates the representation of arithmetic expressions as trees. Note that the placement of parentheses in the expression of Figure 5.9(b) is implied by the tree

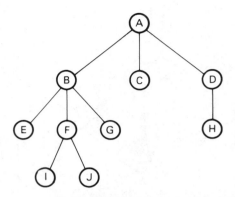

FIGURE 5.7(b)   A Typical Tree

The root of the tree is A. The root A has three subtrees whose roots are B, C, and D. These nodes are the sons of A. Node E is the son of node B and a grandson of A. Node D is the great-uncle of node I. Terminal nodes are C, E, G, H, I, and J.

structure, but that the parentheses themselves need not be included in the tree. Compilers sometimes build tree structures as they scan an expression. Once the tree has been constructed, the translation from tree to object code is fairly straightforward.

5.4.3   Binary Trees

Another information structure much like a tree is the *binary tree*. In a binary tree, each node may have no more than two sons, and a distinction is made between the left son and the right son. A binary tree may be empty, while a tree may not. (There is nothing magic about this distinction, by the way. It's just that the mathematical theory of trees and binary trees works out more conveniently with this distinction.)

Note that the trees in Figure 5.9 are also binary trees. This is not surprising since all of the operations performed in the expressions use binary operators. (What would be the case if one of the expressions contained a ternary operator; that is, one that operates on three operands?) The tree in Figure 5.7(b) is not a binary tree since node A, for example, has three sons.

It is particularly easy to represent a binary tree in a computer memory since we will need, at most, two pointers for each node of the binary tree. (See Figure 5.10.) We will encounter the binary tree again when we discuss the *treesort* method of ordering data items.

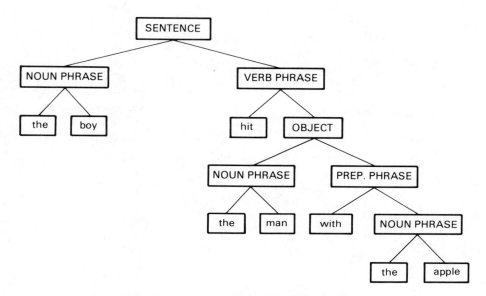

(a) Sentence parse of "The boy hit the man with the apple." Here the man has an apple; the boy hit him.

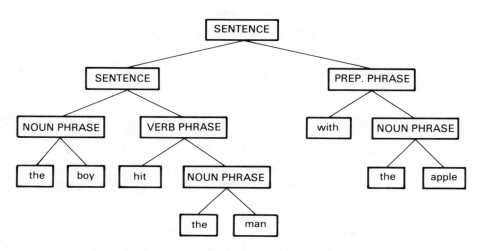

(b) Another parse of the same sentence. The boy bounced an apple off the man.

FIGURE 5.8   Sentence Parsing Using Trees

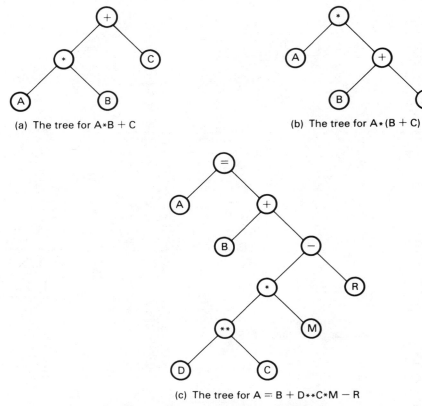

(a) The tree for A∗B + C

(b) The tree for A∗(B + C)

(c) The tree for A = B + D∗∗C∗M − R

FIGURE 5.9   Arithmetic Expressions as Trees

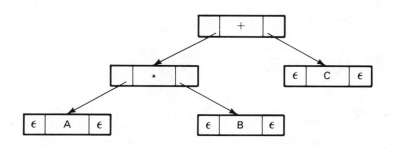

FIGURE 5.10   The Storage Structure Representation of Figure 5.9(a).

5.5 SUMMARY

It should now be apparent that a wealth of information structures lies beyond the humble memory cell. Each kind of structure has its own costs and conveniences, allowing for the efficient representation and processing of certain forms of information. The great advantage to knowing and becoming comfortable with a variety of data structures is similar to the benefit of knowing a number of programming languages. Given a particular problem, we can pick and choose among structures and techniques, tailoring our approach to the problem at hand. The effort on our part will be a minimum and the power of our solution as great as possible.

EXERCISES

Terms You Should Know . . .

Binary Tree	Pop Up
Circular List	Push Down
Data Structure	Queue
Double Linked List	Stack
FIFO	Storage Structure
Graph	Table
Hashing	Terminal Node
LIFO	Tree
Linear List	Value as Index
Linked List	

Basic Skills

1. Taking each of the letters in S-T-O-P in sequence, we can transform the word into O-P-T-S using a stack:

Push (S)	(stack contains: S)
Push (T)	(stack contains: T-S)
Push (O)	(stack contains: O-T-S)
Pop	(stack contains: T-S) (output so far is O)
Push (P)	(stack contains: P-T-S) (output so far is O)
Pop	(stack contains: T-S) (output so far is O-P)
Pop	(stack contains: S) (output so far is O-P-T)
Pop	(stack empty) (final output is O-P-T-S)

a. Starting with the same input, use a stack to transform S-T-O-P to P-O-T-S and to T-O-P-S

b. Find a letter sequence, made of the letters S-T-O-P, into which S-T-O-P can *not* be transformed using a stack. (The sequence need not necessarily form an English word.)

2. What words can you transform S-T-O-P into, using a *queue* rather than a stack?

3. What would be the simplest data structure and storage structure to use for the pool of available words, in the dynamic storage allocation scheme of section 5.3.3?

4. In the quotation from *Through the Looking Glass* at the beginning of the chapter, the Walrus and the Carpenter state that they can only go walking with four Oysters, "to give a hand to each." What kind of data structure does this suggest? What kind of structure is suggested by the last two verses of the quotation?

5. Look at Figure 5.7(a)
   a. What nodes are adjacent to node x_1?
   b. What nodes are connected to node x_1?
   c. Is the graph a connected graph? Why or why not?
   d. What is the largest loop in this graph? (No node may appear in a loop more than once.)
   e. What is the shortest path that connects x_1 with x_2? What is the shortest path that connects x_2 with x_1?

6. Look at the tree of Figure 5.7(b).
   a. What are the subtrees of node B?
   b. What are node B's siblings (that is, brothers and sisters)?
   c. What is the nearest common ancestor of nodes J and C?
   d. What is the relationship between nodes A and J?
   e. True or False: All terminal nodes of a tree must be each other's siblings or first cousins.

7. Diagram this sentence two different ways, using Figure 5.8 as a guide:

   "I swim in the pond with the ducks."

   (*Hint*: In one case "with the ducks" tells us who I swim with. In the other, "with the ducks" specifies which pond I swim in.)

8. Look at Figures 5.5(a) and 5.5(d) which show a sequentially allocated list before and after the deletion of a value. *After* the deletion, what value can probably be found in location 1048?

9. Draw trees to diagram the arithmetic expressions below:

   a. $A = B + C^*(D - E)$
   b. $K = L + SIN(J) + MAX(M,N,P)$
   c. Polish suffix: $QR + CD - ^*$

10. What are the advantages of a double-linked list over a single-linked list? What are the disadvantages?
11. What are the advantages of a circular list over one which is not circular? What are the disadvantages?

Intermediate Problems and Extended Concepts

12. In the sequential allocation of a queue, we said that a list of length L could hold a maximum of $L-1$ items. Why only $L-1$? (*Hint*: What is true about pointers F and R when the list is empty?)
13. Assume that we store information in a table using a hashing scheme. On later lookups, how do we discover that an item we seek is not in the table?
14. A completely filled out binary tree of n levels (that is, all nodes except those in the n-th (bottom) row have two sons; the n-th row nodes have no sons) is composed of $2^n - 1$ nodes. Devise a scheme that uses $2^n - 1$ contiguous words of storage for such a binary tree and that correctly associates nodes with their parents or descendents without using any pointer fields.
15. When, for practical purposes, will the nodes of a linked list require *no more* space than the nodes of a sequentially allocated list?

Suggestions for Computer Programs

1. In a priority interrupt system, an executing task can be interrupted and suspended by a more urgent (higher priority) task. When this happens, the status of the interrupted task is saved on a stack and the interrupting task is executed. When the interrupting task is complete, the system resumes with the task at the top of the stack. Interrupting tasks can also be interrupted by tasks with even higher priority. Develop a program that supervises tasks of this kind, pushing and popping task status information onto/from a stack as required.
2. Create a dynamic storage allocator that serves multiple lists. Use your dynamic allocator in a program that indexes text (i.e., looks through textual material and records the page numbers on which particular words and phrases appear) or cross-references a computer program (i.e., looks through a program listing and records the line numbers on which variable names appear).

3. Set up a modest information system (say containing personal data on the people in your class) using (a) a single linked list; (b) a double linked list; (c) a double linked circular list. The system should include capabilities to add/delete/change/find records and extract information for listing from a record found. Report on the relative advantages and disadvantages of each storage scheme.

"Found *what*?" said the Duck.

"Found *it*," the Mouse replied rather crossly: "of course you know what 'it' means."

"I know what 'it' means well enough when *I* find a thing," said the Duck: "it's generally a frog or a worm."

Lewis Carroll, *Alice in Wonderland,* Chapter 3

"Rule Forty-two. All persons more than a mile high to leave the court."

"That's not a regular rule," said Alice. "You invented it just now."

"It's the oldest rule in the book," said the King.

"Then it ought to be Number One," said Alice.

Lewis Carroll, *Alice in Wonderland,* Chapter 12

6

SEARCHING AND SORTING

6.1 "BUTTON BUTTON, WHO'S GOT THE BUTTON?"

Now that we've got all sorts of interesting ways to pack information away, what are we going to do with it?

Well, for one thing, we can get that information back again. We can look things up, perform calculations, and make decisions based on what we find. The first part of this chapter involves ways of doing the looking up. The second part will show some methods of arranging our data so that lookups can be conveniently performed.

6.2 SEARCHING

We have already seen a couple of techniques for getting information out of a table. The unpacked table of Section 5.2.2 gave a very simple access method, applicable in the case where a value in the row we want to access could be used as an index to the table. The hashing scheme of Section 5.2.3 provided another table access method, although not so simple this time. Both of these schemes revolved around extreme conditions on the value set: the first, that the possible range of values is very small and the actual selection of values is a large percentage of the possible ones; the second that these conditions are exactly reversed.

6.2.1 Serial Search

Now, what about standard, garden variety tables? The most common case is a table of medium length, with the rows arranged so that some column is in order (for example, the part-number column of Figure 5.2). We call the items in this column *keys*, since they serve the special function of distinguishing and identifying table rows. To look up a particular item, we simply search along the table until we find the row containing the key we want, or until we find a key that is greater than the key of the item being sought. In this case, we immediately know that the item looked for is not in the table, since the remaining, unexamined keys will be still larger in value. (See Figure 6.1.)

On average, to find an item or discover that it is not in the table, we would expect to search about halfway down. Sometimes, the search will be longer, sometimes shorter, but on the average, a look-up will require N/2 examinations for a list of length N. This assumes, of course, that there is no special bias in our data. If low numbered parts were

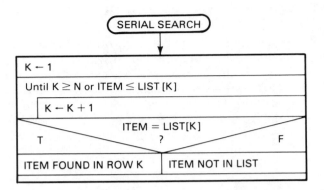

FIGURE 6.1   Flowchart for a Serial Search.

ITEM is the value to be looked up in LIST, which is N rows long. The entries in LIST are assumed to be in ascending order.

looked up most often, we would expect the average search to take less than N/2 examinations.

The principal virtue of the serial search is that it is very easy to program. With a slight modification, it can be used even when the list being searched is not in order. (What is the modification?) The serial search is foolproof.

6.2.2   Binary Search

None of us, however, is a fool, and we can do much better than a serial search. Assuming again that the key column is in order, a *binary search* can speed up the searching process considerably. The basic idea is to compare the item we're looking for against the middle key in the list. If they are equal, we're done. If our item is larger than the middle key, we can throw away the low half of the list and consider only the high half for further examination; vice-versa if our item is smaller than the middle key. We choose the middle entry of the remaining part of the list for comparison, and continue on, halving the quantity of list entries under consideration at each stage. Eventually, this will narrow down to a single entry. Either its key matches our item, or the item must not be present in the list. Given a list of length N, we can halve this list only $\log_2 N$ times (or the next highest integer, if N is not an exact power of 2). This means we will have to make at most $\log_2 N$ examinations to look up our item. Figure 6.3 compares the number of examinations for the serial and binary search.

In practice, the difference is not quite this dramatic. The binary search mechanism is somewhat more complicated than that of the serial search and requires operations that take somewhat longer to perform. (See Figure 6.2.)

The author wrote machine language programs for both a serial and binary search, against a table of length 500 containing the even numbers from 2 to 1000. Each of the integers 0,1,2, . . . ,1000 was looked up in the table. Thus, about half were found and half not, and the distribution of numbers sought was very even. This is a Very Average Case. Two runs were made that were identical except that in the first a serial search was performed, and in the second a binary search. The serial search routine was nine instructions long and the binary search routine was 20 instructions long. By actual count, the process took 1,764,652 machine cycles using the serial search, and 323,667 cycles using the binary search, a ratio of better than five to one. Some program tuning would undoubtedly improve this ratio in favor of the binary search.

In any case, the point is that for searching large tables, the modest effort and tiny amount of extra space that have to be expended for a

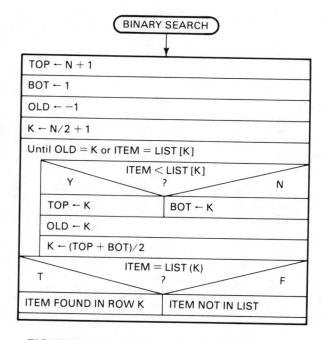

FIGURE 6.2   Flowchart for a Binary Search.

LIST is the same as in Figure 6.1. The divide operation "/" discards any fractional remainder.

Number of List Entries N	Average Number of Examinations in Serial Search N/2	"Worst Case" for Binary Search log₂N*
2	1	1
4	2	2
16	8	4
512	256	9
4,096	2,048	12
32,768	16,384	15

*The logarithm, base 2, of N is the power you have to raise 2 to, to get the value of N. (Try reading that out loud!) Thus $\log_2 64 = 6$ since $2^6 = 64$ and $\log_2 512 = 9$ since $2^9 = 512$. Logs base 2 are similar to common (base 10) and natural (base e) logarithms, in that if N is not an exact power of the base, then log of N is not integral. Thus, for example, $\log_2 10 = 3.32+$.

FIGURE 6.3   Comparison of the Number of Examinations for a List of Length N, Using Serial and Binary Search.

binary search are well worth the trouble. Some languages (notably American National Standard Cobol), have built-in facilities for binary searches, making the use of the technique an even easier choice.

6.2.3   Formula-Address Calculation Search

So far, we have made no assumptions about the contents of the table, except that its entries are in order, and we have been searching rather blindly. If we know something about the numbers in the table—in particular, how they are distributed and in what range they fall—we can perform a *formula* or *address calculation search*. The basic idea is to use our knowledge of the entries to make an intelligent guess as to where a particular number lies.

Suppose we had a table of length 100, and that the 100 entries are drawn randomly from among the numbers 1 to 1000 and sorted in ascending order. Knowing only this, it would be reasonable to guess that the entries whose values range between 1 and 500 will lie in the first half of the table and that the entries which range from 501 to 1000 would lie in the last half of the table. If we had to look up the number 750 in the table, a reasonable place to begin looking is three-fourths of the way up the table (that is, 750/1000 of the way up). This would be entry number 75 of the table. It is altogether probable that 750 will not be *exactly* in LIST[75] but we would expect it at least not to be far away if it is in the table at all.

In general, if the entries are distributed fairly uniformly in the range J to K in a table of length N, a good guess for the row to be accessed first in looking up ITEM is

$$ROW = N*(ITEM - J)/(K - J)$$

Of course, if the entries are not uniformly distributed, this formula will not work very well. Other kinds of distributions are trickier to deal with, but techniques do exist for producing a formula for just about any distribution, all of varying degrees of complexity. Given a function that tells us about where in the range an item falls [f(item) = .6 would mean look six-tenths of the way up in the table] we can multiply by N, the number of entries in the table, to get our initial guess for the row:

$$ROW = N*f(ITEM)$$

If we find that ITEM is less than LIST[ROW], we search downward through the table, otherwise upwards. (See Figure 6.4.) For very large tables and with a good formula, this scheme can be even better than a binary search.

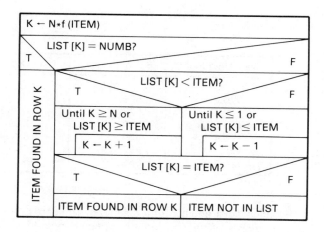

FIGURE 6.4 Flowchart for Formula-Address Calculation Search

6.3   SORTING

By now, the frequent desirability of having a table in order should be fairly clear. Nearly all of the search methods of the last section required order. When we generate output, we often want the information to be ordered in some fashion. Even if a compiler uses a hashing scheme to store symbols, a programmer wants the symbol table listing to be alphabetized. And, consider what a nuisance it would be to have a sales tax table in which the amounts were in no particular order.

In addition, certain kinds of calculations are made more accurate by treating the data in order. (See Figure 6.5.)

6.3.1   Radix Sorting

Sometimes, it is possible to sort our data, before it ever gets near the computer, by using a card sorting machine. This (now slightly antique) machine looks at a specified column on each card and drops it into a particular card pocket depending on what is punched in that column. To sort numbers, we first sort the cards by the column containing the least significant digit. We gather up the contents of the pockets in order and run them through the sorter again, looking at the next most significant digit. This process is repeated as many times as there are columns of information. After the final gathering of cards, the deck is in order. (See Figure 6.6.) You might try hand simulating this process with a pack of playing cards, using face value for one column and suit for another. This

Data Unordered	Running Total	Data Ordered	Running Total
.955	.955	.352	.352
575.	576.	.478	.830
2.36	578.	.955	1.78
.352	578.	2.36	4.14
18.4	596.	18.4	22.5
256.	852.	256.	278.
.478	852.	575.	853.

FIGURE 6.5

Floating point addition of a column of numbers in a computer with a three decimal digit register. The true sum of the numbers is 853.545. Adding the numbers in ascending order improves accuracy by keeping the running total closer in magnitude to the next number to be added, thus minimizing the error due to round-off.

*		*		*		
948	→	321	→	505	→	067
321		124		321		124
849		505		124		227
124		776		227		321
067		946		946		505
776		067		948		776
505		227		849		849
946		948		067		946
227		849		776		948

FIGURE 6.6   Radix Sort

At each step, the list is to be sorted by the column marked by the asterisk, proceeding from least to most significant.

method is called *radix sorting*. It can be programmed for internal sorting and can be a useful approach when the sort key is composed of several table columns (e.g., age and salary).

6.3.2   Exchange Sorting

The simplest way to sort a table stored in memory is to look for the largest element; place it in the last row of the table, shoving the rest of the items up one slot; look for the largest element among the remaining $N-1$ elements, and so on.

The way we actually do this is to examine successive pairs of numbers in the table (the first and second, the second and third, etc.) and exchange them if they are out of order. The first time through the table, the largest entry will drop to the bottom. (Try it.) Then we start back at the top of the table and repeat the procedure. This time, however, we do not need to compare the $N-1$st and Nth entries, since we already know that the Nth element is largest. So, on each pass through the table, we make one fewer comparison until all the entries are sorted. (See Figure 6.7.)

Note that on the first pass we needed to make $N-1$ comparisons, on the second $N-2$ comparisons, etc., for a total of $1+2+\ldots+(N-1) = N(N-1)/2 = (N^2-N)/2$ comparisons altogether. The most significant term in this expression is N^2 and this kind of sort is said to be "of order N^2." What this means is that the time required to sort a list increases roughly as the *square* of the number of items in the list. If we *double* the list size, we *quadruple* the sort time. If it takes 25 seconds to sort 10,000 numbers, it will take about 2,500 seconds (about 40 minutes) to sort 100,000 numbers. Obviously, this kind of sort can be used only if the list size is not too large.

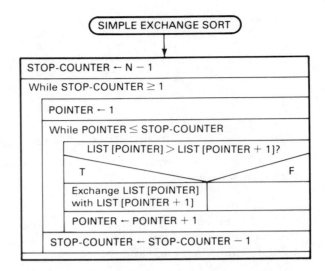

FIGURE 6.7   Simple Exchange Sort

This algorithm and the ones that follow assume the existence of an unordered table called LIST with N rows. For purposes of the examples, the rows are assumed to contain only the numbers to be sorted. In general, the table could contain other columns. Then the comparison would be between   KEY [POINTER] and KEY [POINTER + 1], where KEY represents the table key information; and, as necessary, entire rows of LIST would be exchanged.

We can make a considerable improvement on the exchange sort by making a simple change in the procedure. We start off just the same, but when a pair of numbers is found out of order, we mark our place and then back up, comparing the smaller of the pair with the number just above. If it is still smaller, we exchange and keep moving backwards until the correct spot for our number is found. The advantage here is that, having moved that item to its correct spot, the table is now in order down to the row where we marked our place. We now continue from this row. When we finally get to the bottom, the table is completely sorted.

Because the small elements seem to "bubble" upward to their correct place, this scheme is called a *bubble sort*. A bubble sort *can* take as long as the simple exchange sort, but only if all the entries start out exactly in reverse order. Typically, some (and on the average half) of the numbers will already be relatively in order and far fewer comparisons must be made. If the table is in order to begin with, only N − 1 comparisons are made altogether. The bubble sort is also of order N^2, but generally outperforms the simple exchange sort. (See Figures 6.8 and 6.9.)

Another simple modification can improve the bubble sort. In the backward scan, we can simply *look* for the spot where our number should go. Once we find it, we shove down all the elements between our item and the spot found and then insert our item into the vacated slot. A little consideration will show that this scheme, called the *linear insertion sort,* saves about two-thirds of the move operations required to place the item in the right spot. (All other operations are the same as the bubble sort.) This is the fastest of our N-squared sorts. (Its algorithm is left as an exercise.)

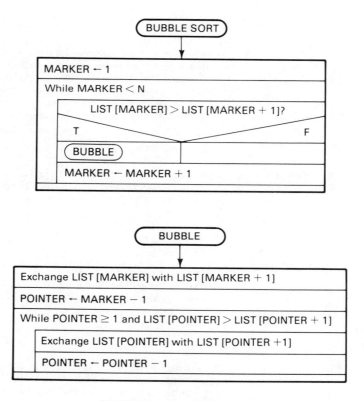

FIGURE 6.8   Bubble Sort

MARKER is the main counter in this algorithm, which moves downward, once, through the table. All numbers above MARKER are in order. POINTER is a subordinate counter. When two numbers are found out of order, POINTER moves upward through the table exchanging the smaller item with larger items above it in the table.

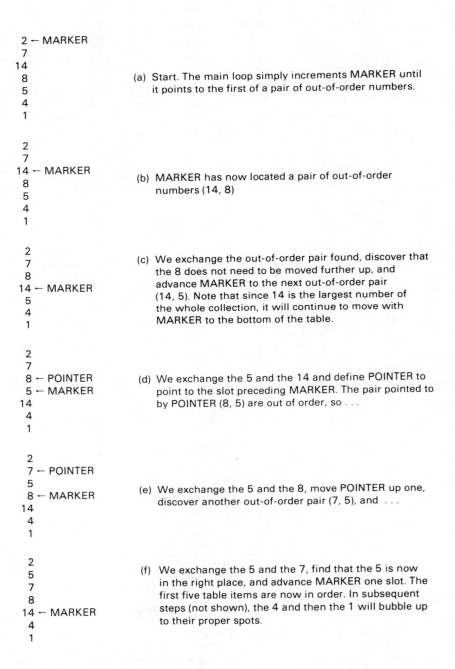

FIGURE 6.9   Partial Example of the Operation of Bubble Sort.

6.3.3 Address Calculation Sorting

If we have a little space to burn, a very neat sorting scheme can be used that makes only a single pass through the original table. This scheme, like the address calculation search, also requires that we know something about the distribution of our numbers and that we can produce an address calculation formula. We set up an empty "target" table and then examine the entries in the original table one by one. Using the formula, we find a "good" spot in the target for the item. If a collision occurs (that is, the formula gives us a row of the target table that is already occupied), we step through the target in the appropriate direction until an empty slot is found. Sometimes, we will find that our item must go between two numbers that are next to each other in the target table. In this case, we must move some of the target's numbers over to make room for our item.

Obviously, the larger we make the target table, the fewer collisions we will have and the less stepping through and shifting around of the target we will have to do. On the other hand, when we have finished the sort, we will want to squeeze out the gaps from the target table so the table is compact again. This squeezing process requires some time and, as the table size increases, so does squeeze time. It has been shown by Flores [4] that the optimal size for the target table is 2.2 times the size of the original table.

6.3.4 Tag Sorting

For sizable tables, many of the sorting schemes above require a considerable amount of data movement, particularly if the table is complex (say made out of several arrays). All of this data moving can be quite a nuisance. An alternative is to only pretend that we move data, and here's how it works:

We set up an array called a *tag array* (or index array) which is as long as the table to be sorted, but which needs only to be wide enough to hold numbers as big as N, the length of the table. Initially we set TAG[1] = 1, TAG[2] = 2, etc. We now use any sorting scheme we like. When we want to refer to the jth table item, we actually refer to TABLE[TAG[j]]. Any moving that needs to be done is performed only on the tag array and not on the table itself. When the sort is complete, TABLE[TAG[1]] will refer to the smallest row of the table, TABLE[TAG[2]] to the next smallest, and so on. (See Figure 6.10.) We don't ever need to shift around the table entries themselves, although this may be desirable once the sort is complete since double-level subscripting is slow (and, in some programming languages, requires some subterfuge).

List to be sorted:

TABLE [1] = 36
TABLE [2] = 41
TABLE [3] = 17
TABLE [4] = 68
TABLE [5] = 55
TABLE [6] = 91
TABLE [7] = 72
TABLE [8] = 84
TABLE [9] = 26

	i	TAG [i]	TABLE [TAG [i]]
Initial Setup:	1	1	36
	2	2	41
	3	3	17
	4	4	68
	5	5	55
	6	6	91
	7	7	72
	8	8	84
	9	9	26
After One Pass of Simple Exchange Sort:	1	1	36
	2	3	17
	3	2	41
	4	5	55
	5	4	68
	6	7	72
	7	8	84
	8	9	26
	9	6	91
After Sort Is complete:	1	3	17
	2	9	26
	3	1	36
	4	2	41
	5	5	55
	6	4	68
	7	7	72
	8	8	84
	9	6	91

FIGURE 6.10   Tag Sort

6.3.5   List Merge-Sort

By now, you are probably wondering what happened to all of those fancy data structures of Chapter 5. The time has come to put some of them to work.

The first technique we'll look at is the *list merge*. Suppose we have two lists, each of which is in order, and we want to combine them to form one ordered list. This is very straightforward. We look at the first element of each list. One of these two entries must be the smallest of all of the elements since both lists are ordered. We pick the smaller element off its list and queue it onto a result list. The second item on the list from which we took the item now moves up to become that list's first entry. We again compare first elements and pick the smaller, and so on, until one of the lists is exhausted. We then tack the rest of the remaining list onto the end of the result list and we're done. (See Figure 6.11.)

Now suppose we have an unsorted list. We can put it in order by using a technique called a *merge-sort*. (See Figure 6.12.) Let's call our initial list I (for initial or input), and set up four lists L1, L2, L3, and L4, all of which are initially empty. The first step is to distribute the items on I between L1 and L2. We copy items from I to L1 so long as the items

(a)			(b)			(c)		
3	4	empty	5	4	3	5	7	3
5	7		9	7		9		4
9			14			14		
14								
LIST 1	LIST 2	RESULT	LIST 1	LIST 2	RESULT	LIST 1	LIST 2	RESULT
(d)			(e)			(f)		
9	7	3	9	empty	3	empty	empty	3
14		4	14		4			4
		5			5			5
					7			7
								9
								14
LIST 1	LIST 2	RESULT	LIST 1	LIST 2	RESULT	LIST 1	LIST 2	RESULT

FIGURE 6.11   List Merge

At each step the smallest item among lists 1 and 2 is picked off and added to the result list. When one of the lists becomes empty, the remainder of the other list is tacked onto the end of the result list.

(a)	(b)		(c)		(d)		(e)
Initial List	L1	L2	L3	L4	L1	L2	L3 (Final List)
13	13	6	6	11	6	3	3
21	21	18	13	48	11	14	6
6	11	49	18	64	13		11
18	64	48	21	71	18		13
49	14	71	49	98	21		14
11		98	3		48		18
64		3	14		49		21
48					64		48
71					71		49
98					98		64
14							71
3							98

(a)   The initial, unsorted list
(a) → (b)   Distribution of initial list onto L1 and L2
(b) → (c)   First merge pass
(c) → (d)   Second merge pass
(d) → (e)   Final merge pass

FIGURE 6.12   List Merge-Sort

are in ascending order. As soon as we encounter an entry on I that is smaller than its predecessor, we switch and begin copying onto L2. When we find the next out-of-order element, we switch back to L1, and go back and forth until I is exhausted.

Now on each of L1 and L2 we have a series of small ordered sublists (each possibly only a few elements long). We take the first sublist on L1 and merge it with the first sublist L2, putting the result on L3. We then merge the second pair of sublists onto L4, the third pair back onto L3, and so on. When L1 and L2 are exhausted, L3 and L4 will each contain a series of sublists, but there will be half as many sublists on L3 and L4 as there were on L1 and L2 and each sublist will be, on average, twice as long as the old sublists.

We now re-merge, going from L3 and L4 to L1 and L2, and back and forth, halving the number of sublists, and doubling their size on each pass. Eventually, we will end up with only a single sublist on each of two of our lists. A final merge pass forms one sorted list and we're done. This may sound rather complicated but a little practice will show that the technique is really quite straightforward and quite quick.

This kind of sort is on the order of $N \cdot \log_2 N$, since we examine (at most) N entries on each pass, and the maximum number of passes needed is $\log_2 N$ (since the number of sublists is halved at each pass). What is also surprising is that the merge-sort can be accomplished using storage space made up of the initial list plus space for *one* additional list of the same size as I. (How?) This makes the merge-sort not only quick but also fairly economical of space.

The merge-sort can be made even faster by using more than two lists at each pass. Begin by spreading the initial list among k lists and, thereafter, perform k-way merges. The order then becomes $N \cdot \log_k N$ (and the bigger k is, the smaller $\log_k N$ becomes). To sort quantities of data larger than the computer's memory, we can substitute magnetic tapes or disks for the internal lists. In this fashion, we can sort millions of numbers fairly efficiently.

6.3.6 Tree Sorts

If both time and space are at a premium, a small programming investment can save us both by using the binary tree data structure. This scheme, first described by Floyd [5] is called a *treesort*. We will examine this sorting method which Floyd called TREESORT3, and then a modification developed by Fisher and Dewar [2] called TREESORT4.

Recall that each node of a binary tree has zero, one, or two sons, and that the sons are called either left son or right son. We will label the nodes of the binary tree as follows:

1. Give the root of the tree the label 1.
2. For any node N, label its left son 2N and its right son $2N + 1$.

Keep in mind that these numbers are only "names" for the nodes and not the contents of the nodes. (The root, labeled 1, might *contain* the number 275.3.) Note that we can find the father of any node (other than the root) simply by dividing its label by 2 and throwing away any fractional remainder.

TREESORT3 has two parts. The first *partially orders* the tree. This means that the contents of each node will be greater than or equal to the contents of its sons. The heart of Part 1 is a recursive procedure called "siftup," which is applied at each call to a single node of the tree:

1. If the node has no sons, or if the node is greater than each of its sons, then return to caller.
2. Otherwise, exchange the node with the larger of its two sons and apply "siftup" to this son (which now has the value of the original node).

We apply "siftup" to each node successively, beginning with the highest labeled node that has sons and proceeding toward the root. Figure 6.13 shows how this process works. (Figures 6.13 and 6.14 are adapted from [2] with the permission of the author.)

Part 2 sorts the tree into ascending order. One result of Part 1 is that the largest value in the tree is now in node 1. We exchange node 1 with the highest labeled node and then "wall it off" from the tree. We have thus found the largest value in the tree and put it aside. Now we resift node 1, leaving the walled-off node out of the sifting process. In this

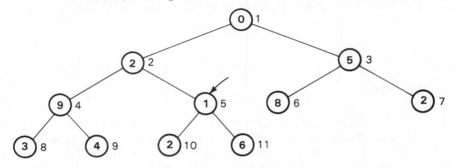

(a) This is the tree to be partially ordered. The highest numbered node with sons is node 5, which contains a 1. This value is smaller than the values of its sons. We exchange with the higher valued son (node 11).

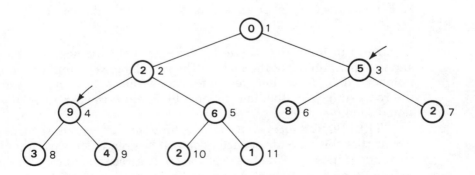

(b) Node 11, which has just been exchanged, has no sons, so we continue down the original list of nodes to node 4. The contents of node 4 are already larger than the contents of both of its sons, so we proceed to node 3. We exchange node 3 with node 6, the larger of its two sons.

FIGURE 6.13   Siftup

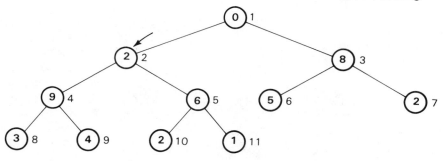

(c) Node 6, which has just been exchanged, has no sons, so we proceed to node 2. Node 2 must be exchanged with node 4, its larger son.

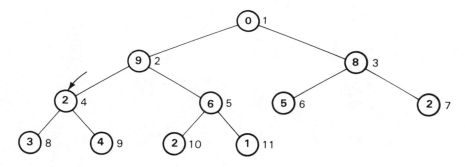

(d) Node 4 does have sons, and must be exchanged with node 9, its larger son. Note that the *value* 2 is working its way down the tree.

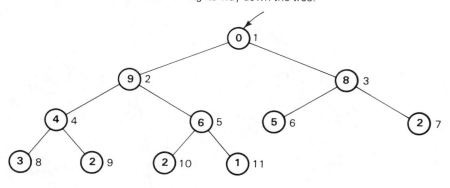

(e) Node 9, which has just been exchanged, has no sons, so we pick up again in the original list of nodes. The only node still to be sifted is node 1, the root. In the next three steps, the *value* 0 sifts from node 1, eventually down to node 10.

FIGURE 6.13 (continued)

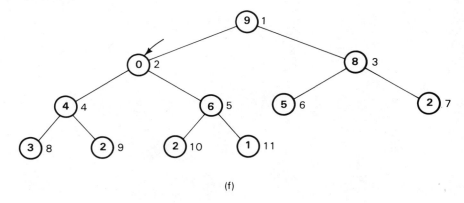

(f)

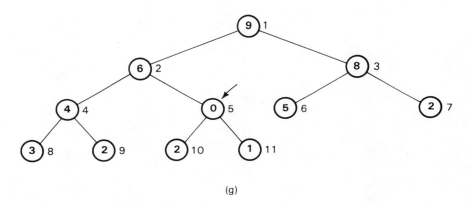

(g)

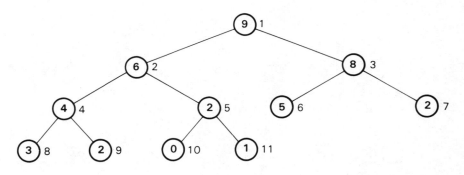

(h) The tree is now partially ordered. Note that if you start at the root and follow any path, the values of the nodes along the path are in order.

FIGURE 6.13 (continued)

manner, the next largest node will end up in node 1. Again we exchange, this time with the highest labeled node not yet walled off, and so on. We continue to exchange and sift, at each pass picking up and walling off the largest remaining value. For a tree with N nodes, after $N-1$ such passes, the tree is completely sorted into ascending order (see Figure 6.14). The order of this sort is $2N(\log_2 N - 1)$.

The speed of this sorting method can be improved considerably if we make a few observations about Part 2. In particular, note that when we exchange node 1 with the highest labeled node, we install a very small value into the root of the tree. When we ask whether this node is larger than each of its sons, the answer will always be "no."

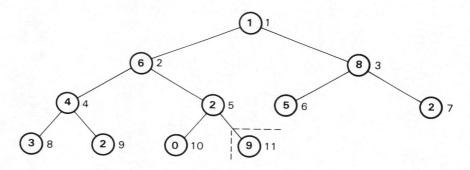

(a) Proceeding from Figure 6.13(h), we exchange nodes 1 and 11, and wall off this last node (which now contains the largest value in the tree). Node 1 must now be resifted.

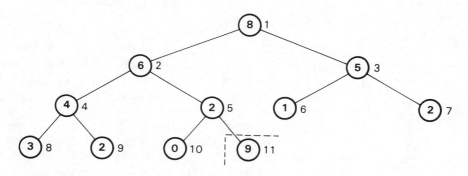

(b) Node 1 has now been sifted down to node 6 and the next highest value now resides in node 1.

FIGURE 6.14   Part 2 of TREESORT3

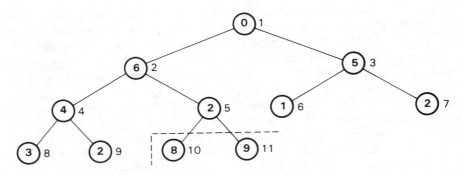

(c) Nodes 1 and 10 are exchanged, and node 10 is walled off. We now have to resift node 1. The sifting, exchanging, and walling off continues until the tree is in order.

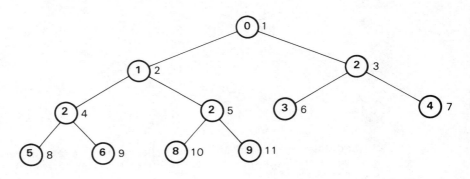

(d) The final, sorted tree.

FIGURE 6.14 (continued)

This being so, we might just as well not ask the question. This will save us two compares at each pass. In addition, since the value in the root came from the bottom of the tree, the likelihood is that we will sift it most of the way back down again. For every level this value is sifted, we use up two compares and a move.

Using these observations, TREESORT4 employs the following scheme. A sift is made through the tree all the way to the bottom. *Ignoring* the value of the root, it simply chooses and moves the larger of the two sons at each level. This requires only *one* comparison at each level (comparing the two sons against each other) rather than two (comparing our value to each son). After reaching the bottom, we then back up the tree until we find the proper spot to put our value. Since this spot is likely to be near the bottom of the tree, not much effort will be wasted. In fact, the number of extra moves is about N/3 on average, but the number of compares is reduced to less than $N \cdot \log_2 N$. This is a substantial improvement over the $2N \cdot \log_2(N-1)$ of TREESORT3, but requires some extra programming.

6.4 SUMMARY

We have seen a variety of searching and sorting methods. The selection is by no means exhaustive, but it is fairly representative. Each of the different methods has its own virtues and deficiencies. Some are short and easy to program, but are slow. Others are fast but require extra storage. Methods that conserve both time and space require considerable ingenuity to program. Given a set of constraints for a project, you should now be in a position to intelligently choose the most appropriate method.

EXERCISES

Terms You Should Know . . .

Address Calculation Search	List Merge-Sort
Address Calculation Sort	$\log_2 N$
Binary Search	Radix Sort
Bubble Sort	Serial Search
Linear Insertion Sort	Simple Exchange Sort
List Merge	Tag Sort
	Tree Sort

Basic Skills

1. Modify Figure 6.1 (the sequential search flowchart) so that it will work correctly even if the numbers are not arranged in order in the table.
2. In Figure 6.1 (the sequential search flowchart), the main loop is partly controlled by the test "$K \geq N$". Why is the weak inequality used to control the loop, rather than the strong inequality "$K > N$"?
3. Rank the three exchange sorts, the list merge-sort, and formula-address calculation sort for speed and (separately) for the memory space they require to hold data.

4. Discuss the similarities and differences between hashing and address-calculation searches and sorts.

5. Perform a list merge on the two ordered lists below:

List 1	List 2
1	12
5	15
9	30
15	40
27	41
34	100

6. Perform a list merge-sort using the following set of input numbers

   a. merging back and forth between *pairs* of lists

   b. merging back and forth between two sets of three lists each (and an initial distribution pass that splits the input three ways).

   Input: 19 27 34 2 4 14 24 8 11 28 92 6 16 26 36 3 15 22 9 35 41

7. Starting with the table:

$$
\begin{array}{c}
1 \\
2 \\
4 \\
5 \\
6 \\
7 \\
8 \\
3
\end{array}
$$

   show what happens after one pass of the simple exchange sort and after one pass of the bubble sort.

8. Devise a formula for an address calculation search for a table of 100 slots which will contain numbers in the range 1 to 1,000 and in which numbers over 500 are twice as likely to appear as numbers 500 or less.

9. Starting with the table:

$$2$$
$$3$$
$$5$$
$$8$$
$$11$$
$$14$$
$$19$$
$$23$$
$$25$$
$$29$$
$$30$$
$$31$$

identify the sequence of numbers *looked at* by the binary search in locating 25 and in attempting to locate 20 (which isn't in the table).

Intermediate Problems and Extended Concepts

10. Modify the simple exchange sort algorithm of Figure 6.7 to handle a multicolumn table, say columns called A, B, and C which contain ordinary information, and column KEY which contains row key information. We want to have the table appear in ascending order of KEY values.

11. Modify the bubble sort algorithm of Figure 6.8 to sort a column of numbers into *de*scending order.

12. Modify the bubble sort algorithm of Figure 6.8 to become a linear insertion sort. (*Hint*: Only routine BUBBLE requires changing.)

13. Devise an algorithm to accomplish a list merge. Using this algorithm as a subprocedure, devise another algorithm which accomplishes the list merge-sort.

14. Devise a storage scheme for the list merge-sort that requires only the space of the original list of numbers and *one* additional list of the same size. Assume that the space used by the original list is reusable. (*Hint*: "My candle burns at both ends . . . It casts a lovely light.")

Suggestions for Computer Programs

1. Implement several of the searching/sorting schemes and verify their relative speeds for a list of 200 numbers.

2. Implement TREESORT3 or TREESORT4 to sort a sequential table of numbers. Note that the father-son relationships are completely handled by the node numbering scheme and that no pointer fields are required.

3. Try the address calculation sort with target tables ranging in size from 100% to 300% of the size of the original table and compare running times.

The twelve jurors were all writing very busily on slates. "What are they doing?" Alice whispered to the Gryphon. "They can't have anything to put down yet, before the trial's begun."

"They're putting down their names," the Gryphon whispered in reply, "for fear they should forget them before the end of the trial."

Lewis Carroll, *Alice in Wonderland*, Chapter 11

"Who cares for you?" said Alice. . . . "You're nothing but a pack of cards!"

Lewis Carroll, *Alice in Wonderland*, Chapter 12

7

DATA MANAGEMENT

7.1 "GIVE ME A DATUM AND PLACE TO STAND, AND I'LL MOVE THE EARTH."

There comes a time in every programmer's career when it is either inconvenient or impossible to keep all of his or her data in the memory of a computer all at once. You are already familiar with this idea if you have ever used a set of data that you processed one line at a time. You read one line, processed it, and then went on to the next, keeping in memory only currently relevant information. When the computer's memory is no longer a sufficient storage device, we expand to other devices that are linked to the computer. This chapter concerns the management of data on these peripheral devices.

Let's begin by agreeing on some terminology. The individual little pieces of data (like name or a number) with which we will deal are called *elementary data items* (or just *items*, for short). A collection of items, usually related in some way, is called a *record* (e.g., the name, sex, major subject, and age of a student). An aggregate of records is called a *file* (the collection of all students on campus). (See Figure 7.1).

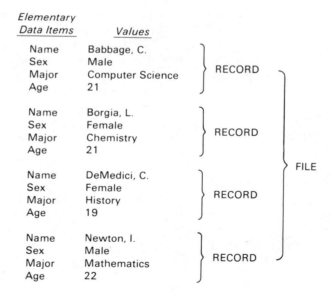

FIGURE 7.1   Items, Records, File

A student file of four records is shown, arranged alphabetically by last name.

7.2 KINDS OF PERIPHERAL DEVICES

Storage devices are broadly classed into three categories. The first and humblest is *unit record*. This category includes printers, display terminals, card readers, punches, etc. These devices are often read-only or write-only. (Attempts to send data *to* a card reader are at best frustrating.) A more distinguishing characteristic is that they generally deal with a fixed quantity of information at a time (e.g., a card, a print line, a line on a screen), hence the name unit record.

The second category is *sequential devices*. These are devices on which information must be retrieved in the same order as it was stored. (What kind of information structure is this?) Tape drives are the principal member of this category. To access the fiftieth record on a tape, we must first pass over the 49 records in front of it. A home tape recorder is a good analogy to this kind of device. To get to a particular song on a tape we can crank the tape recorder forward as fast as it will go till our selection is reached, but there is no way to jump directly to the fifth song. (See Figure 7.2.)

In contrast, if we are playing a phonograph record, we can pick up the arm and (gently) place it anywhere on the record we care to listen. The category of devices analogous to this is called *direct access* and principally includes disks and drums.

A *disk* is composed of one or more flat plates covered with a magnetic oxide (much like the coating on magnetic tape) that spin around very rapidly (see Figure 7.3). Poised over each plate is a read/write head that combines the traits of a tape deck head and a phonograph arm, for it may be moved in and out very quickly to access any track on the plate. A track is analogous to a groove on a record. However, disk tracks are

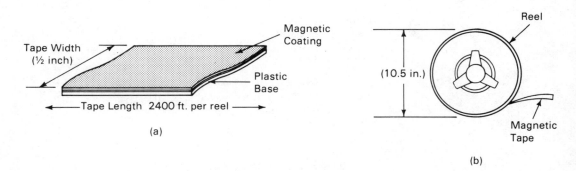

Tape Width (½ inch)

Magnetic Coating

Plastic Base

Tape Length 2400 ft. per reel

(a)

(10.5 in.)

Reel

Magnetic Tape

(b)

FIGURE 7.2 Magnetic Tape

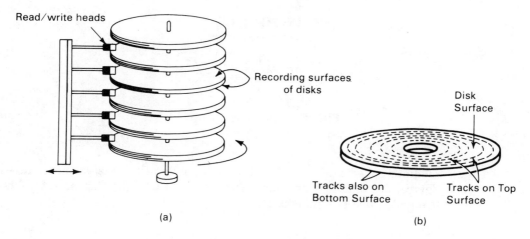

Read/write heads

Recording surfaces of disks

Disk Surface

Tracks also on Bottom Surface

Tracks on Top Surface

(a)

(b)

FIGURE 7.3   The Disk

concentric circles, not one long spiral as on a record. To access the information on a particular track, we first position the head and then wait for the beginning of our data to pass under the head.

The head movement is called a *seek* and it is about the slowest operation a disk can perform, taking on the order of a tenth of a second. The wait for information to come under the read/write head is called *latency* or *rotational delay*. This delay averages half the disk's rotation time thus, typically, a much smaller fraction of a second than the seek delay.

A *drum* (see Figure 7.4) is a cylinder (like a soup can, although bigger), with magnetic oxide on the outside, that spins on its axis. Information appears as tracks that are circles on the outside of the cylinder. Typically, though not always, drums come with a separate read/write head for each of these tracks, eliminating the need for (and the wait due to) seeking. Drums subject us only to rotational delay. However, drums generally hold far less information than disks and the proliferation of read/write heads makes the drum considerably more expensive than a disk, per million characters of information held.

Direct access devices *can* be used as sequential devices (you can after all, begin playing a record at the beginning, and listen through till the end) and often are, depending on the particular application.

As always, there are trade-offs in our choice of devices. Tapes can hold the most information but tend to be relatively slow to access, especially if we are interested in a particular item buried in the middle of our data. The drum is fastest but holds the least. The disk is of inter-

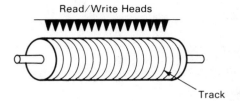

Read/Write Heads

Track

FIGURE 7.4   The Drum

mediate speed and capacity. Computer memory is also a direct access device, the smallest and most expensive, but by far the fastest. (What kind of device is a jukebox?)

7.3   LOGICAL ORGANIZATION

7.3.1   Sequential Organization

The easiest way to arrange records on a storage medium is sequentially, regardless of the kind of access available. Generally, one data item in each record is chosen as a means to order the records (e.g., last name or zip code), and is called a *key*. Your student directory and the typical office filing cabinet are examples of sequential organization.

Now the thing we do most often to a file is change it. A student changes addresses, another drops out of school, two new students enroll. Making changes to a sequential file can sometimes be difficult. To insert a new record we must, in effect, push others aside to make room. When a record is deleted, the gap created must be closed up. Usually, it is economical to update a sequential file only when a number of changes have accumulated. Generally, we write a new copy of the entire file as we go, making the changes along the way.

The principal virtue of a sequential file is that it is easy to get to the "next" record. This is a useful feature and should not be discounted; however, if a file must frequently be updated, other forms of organization may be more appropriate.

7.3.2   Random Organization

Random organization depends on being able to take a key and transform it into an address on our device. Sometimes (not very often), this information is already known and we can simply pass the address along to the device to have it retrieve our record.

More often, a *directory* is used that contains only the key of a record and its file address. To locate an item, we search the directory for the key (using any of our search methods), pick up the file address, and access our record. (See Figure 7.5.) Often, the directory is compact enough to fit into memory and may be searched very conveniently. Sometimes, however, a directory becomes so large that it will not fit into memory or that searching through it becomes impractical. In this case, a slightly more sophisticated scheme must be employed. One such scheme is a multilevel directory. For a name and address file, we might have 26 separate directories, one for each letter of the alphabet, and a 27th directory to act as a guide to the other 26. To look up John Doe's record, we first use only his last initial as a key. We look through our guide to find where the D directory is stored, bring that directory only into memory, and then look up Mr. Doe's complete last name to find the address of his record. (See Figure 7.6. Can you think of a simple generalization that would break an alphabetic key up into more than 26 parts?)

A scheme that does without directories is one in which the key is an argument to some function whose value is a file address. This is a variation on hashing functions and is subject to the same advantages and difficulties.

7.3.3   List Organization

It may have already occurred to you that one way to get around the updating difficulties of a sequential file is to build our file in the form of a linked list. Insertions and deletions are now easy—all we have to do is modify a few pointers. Figure 7.7 shows a student file linked together.

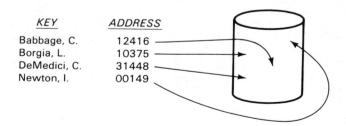

KEY	*ADDRESS*
Babbage, C.	12416
Borgia, L.	10375
DeMedici, C.	31448
Newton, I.	00149

FIGURE 7.5   Directory Look-Up

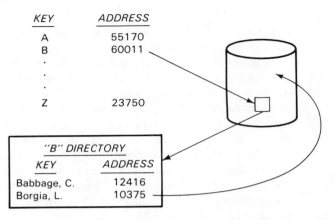

FIGURE 7.6   **Two-Level Directory Look-Up**

To get the record for Ms. Borgia, we first fetch the "B" directory and then look up her entire name.

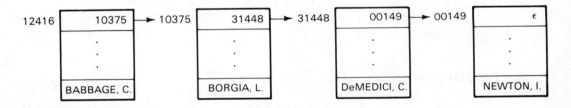

FIGURE 7.7   **Logical Sequential File**

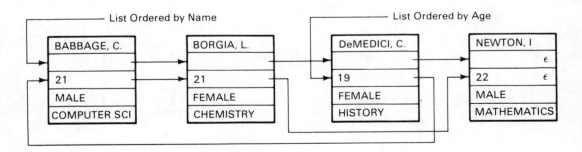

FIGURE 7.8   **File Ordered in Two Ways**

The entries can be treated as though they were arranged in alphabetic order, even though *physically* they are scattered all over the storage medium. This type of structure is called *logical sequential.*

Once we have started a list structure, small modifications can make the structure much more flexible. We can, for example, use more than one key as the basis for connecting our list. In addition to the alphabetic ordering, by adding another pointer to each record, we can also order the list by the ages of the students (see Figure 7.8) or any other key we choose.

It would also be handy to have lists of everyone with the same value for a particular data item (e.g., all math majors, all chemistry majors, all the men, all the women, etc.). We *could* form lists as above and then trace through the list until we came to the math major part of the file. There are two disadvantages to this scheme. The first is that we may have to walk through a lot of list before we get to the part we want. (Looking up zoology students would be awfully time consuming.) The second is that for each of the (possibly several hundred) math majors, the value MATH is repeated, which is a waste of space. One way around this is to combine the directory idea with linked lists.

For example, for the data item SEX there are only the values MALE and FEMALE. In our directory, we enter the item "SEX," and for each of the two possible values, we *point to a linked list* which contains only those records that correspond to that value (see Figure 7.9). We have two disjoint linked lists now, one of the men and one of the women. Observe that we can tell the sex of a student simply by virtue of which list his or her record is on. This being so, we can remove the word MALE or FE-MALE from each record. This process is called *partially inverting the list* with respect to a data item. We can do the same thing with major subjects and with ages. (While this potentially saves a lot of space, it is not without its disadvantages. What are they?)

This process can be carried one step further to *complete list inversion,* in which all links are removed. For each data value, we develop and store *a sequential list of addresses* of records that contain the value. The principal advantage of complete inversion is speed in finding records that must meet several conditions. For example, to find records of female students who are 21 years old (presuming that sex and age are completely inverted), we simply compare lists of record addresses. If an address appears in the list of females and in the list of 21-year-olds, we set the address aside for selection (see Figure 7.10). Note that this process involves no accesses at all to the file until we are ready to pick up the actual records. The cost, of course, is that inverted lists require substantial space in memory.

It is possible to partially or completely invert a list with respect to any data we feel like, but this is not always desirable. We would *not* want

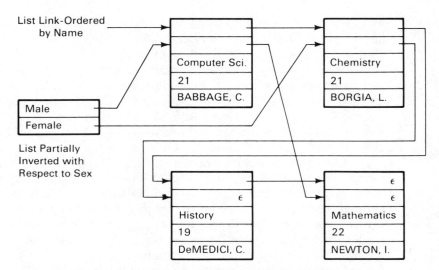

FIGURE 7.9 Link Ordered and Partially Inverted List

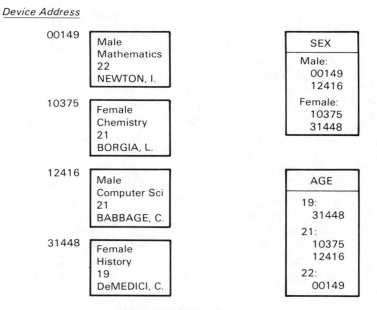

FIGURE 7.10 Complete Inversion

To find all students who are female and 21 years of age, we compare the appropriate lists from each collection. We find that the record at address 10375 meets both criteria. This is all done before actually accessing the file at all.

to invert the list with respect to names, for instance, since we would probably end up with several thousand lists, each only a couple of entries long.

7.3.4   Indexed Organization

A very popular combination of sequential and random organization is called *indexed* organization. In indexed organization, data records are arranged sequentially on a direct access device in a series of *blocks* (where each block represents a fixed amount of space and typically contains several records). We build a directory that contains the key and location of the first record of each block (see Figure 7.11).

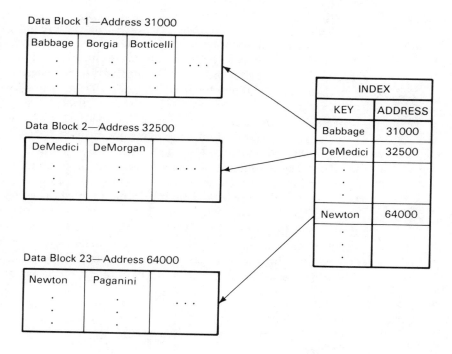

FIGURE 7.11   Indexed File Organization

To locate a record, we determine which two index keys surround the key we want and access the block addressed by the smaller surrounding key. Alternatively, we can read the whole file sequentially.

In this manner, we can read the file sequentially, ignoring the directory, or use the directory to locate the block that contains our record. Once we have the block in hand, finding the record we want is quick and easy.

There are some complications when we add or delete records from the file. If the first record of a block is deleted, or a new record is placed at the beginning of a block, corresponding adjustments have to be made to the directory. If *all* records of a block are deleted, the directory must be adjusted. If a record is added that will not fit into a block (all available space in the block already used by existing records) we have to find a place to put the record.

One scheme takes records from the end of a too-large data block, puts them into a special *overflow area,* and sets a bit in the main data block. Then, when we search for a record, we start by looking in its usual block. If the search key is larger than the last record's key in this block *and* the overflow bit is on, then we also look in the overflow area before giving up.

All of these mechanics are generally handled automatically by standard system software and do not represent a headache to the programmer. (*You* just do a Read.) However, an indexed file that has many records in the overflow area can be relatively slow to access (since multiple searches must be made for many records). To cure this, we will occasionally reorganize an indexed file by writing all of its records out in order on tape. We then read them back in, recreating the indexed file and directory, but now without any overflow records. Often, during reorganization, we will specify that some extra space be left in each data block to permit some amount of expansion of the file without causing overflow.

An alternative indexed scheme links the data blocks *logically* rather than physically, while still maintaining a keyed directory of the individual blocks. To read such a file sequentially, we read the records of the first block in order, then follow a link to the second block and read *its* records, and so on. Now, when a block overflows, we can split it more or less evenly into *two* blocks, store them separately (linking both blocks into the overall block chain), and update the directory appropriately.

7.3.5   And So Forth

There are a number of other schemes for organizing files, some of which are fairly esoteric. For each kind of data structure mentioned in Chapter 5, there is an analogous file design and, as before, each has its particular advantages and drawbacks.

7.4 INFORMATION TRANSMISSION

As a final topic in this chapter, we will take a brief look at some schemes to assist the quick and accurate transmission of information between memory and peripherals. For example purposes, we will concentrate on magnetic tape, which seems to be the easiest storage medium to visualize. The principles involved hold for all kinds of devices.

7.4.1 Parity Checking

In using computers, we tend to read, write, and reread information in vast quantities. The ability to do this with speed and precision is, in fact, one of the great powers of a data processing device. Now, it is not too hard for people to understand and interpret information that has pieces missing or incorrect. Take the following sentence in which "x" replaces all vowels:

Thxs sxntxncx xs nxt txx hxrd tx rxxd.

The computer, however, cannot make effective use of context or intuition without elaborate (and error prone) programming. This is even more true for numeric data. It is extremely important, therefore, that the computer be letter perfect when it reads and writes information and do its best to discover cases when things have gone wrong.

Information on a tape is arranged in a series of parallel *tracks* (see Figure 7.12(a)) that run the length of the tape. Each track is a string of bits. A column of these bits (i.e., one from each track) forms a character. For computers that use a six-bit character, we might expect to find six tracks on a tape. In fact, there is an extra track, used for error detection, called a *parity track*. (*Parity* means oddness or evenness.) Similarly, computers with eight-digit characters will use nine-track tapes.

Let's suppose we wanted our tape to have even parity—i.e., an even number of 1 bits in each column of information. (It doesn't matter whether we pick even or odd, as long as we are consistent. In any particular system, this choice will be predefined.) We achieve this by using a bit from the parity track for each character.

If the six information bits of a character already have an even number of 1's, we make the corresponding parity bit a zero to keep the total even. If the six information bits have an odd number of 1's, we make the parity bit 1 to force an even total. This is all done automatically, by the way, at the point that the tape is written and each character is immediately reread by the device to make sure it went out correctly.

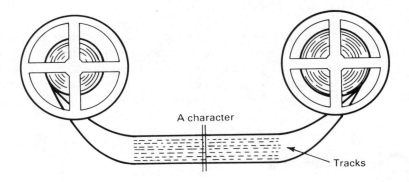

A character

Tracks

FIGURE 7.12(a)

Information is arranged on the surface of a magnetic tape in a series of parallel lines called *tracks*. A character is made up of a column of bits, one from each track.

When the tape is read back, the device counts up the 1's in each character. If the total is *odd* in any character, then some bit of the character has gotten altered. This can be caused by a bad magnetic spot on the tape or even by a speck of dust. We can report this condition, for handling by the system or by the programmer. This scheme is called *single error detecting* since we can determine for any character if one bit has gone bad, although we can't tell which bit.

We can do better than this by also sticking an additional "character" at the end of a specified group of characters to form a parity check on the tracks. If the information part of the track has an even number of 1's, we leave a zero in the corresponding track of the check character; otherwise, we install a one. (This is called *longitudinal parity checking*.)

Now if a bit gets mashed, we know what character the error is in by use of the parity track. We also know what track it is in by use of the longitudinal parity check. This exactly pinpoints the bit in error. Since a bit only has two possible values, if we know that a bit is wrong, then we also know how to fix it. This scheme is called *single error correcting* (see Figure 7.12(b)).

7.4.2 Blocking and Buffering

In the ancient days of long ago (say 1957), input and output (I/O) were handled directly by a computer's central processing unit (CPU). When a command was issued to transfer data between memory and a peripheral

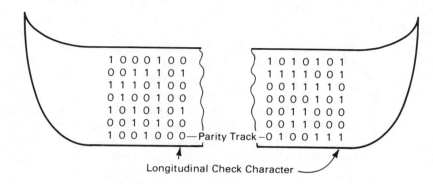

```
1 0 0 0 1 0 0                    1 0 1 0 1 0 1
0 0 1 1 1 0 1                    1 1 1 1 0 0 1
1 1 1 0 1 0 0                    0 0 1 1 1 1 0
0 1 0 0 1 0 0                    0 0 0 0 1 0 1
1 0 1 0 1 0 1                    0 0 1 1 0 0 0
0 0 1 0 1 0 0                    0 0 1 1 0 0 0
1 0 0 1 0 0 0—Parity Track—0 1 0 0 1 1 1
```

Longitudinal Check Character

FIGURE 7.12(b)   Parity Checking

Two sequences of characters are displayed, as they might appear on magnetic tape. The bottom row in each sequence is the parity track and the last column in each is the longitudinal check character. The first example is correct, but there is a single error in the second. Can you find it?

device, processing had to wait until this command was completed. Since activities involving peripherals are slow relative to internal processing speeds, it was quickly recognized that an alternative scheme was necessary.

This led to the development of the *data channel*—a small, rather stupid subcomputer completely under the control of the CPU. Now, when I/O is to be performed, the CPU passes the command to the data channel. The channel has access both to memory and the peripherals and performs the data transfer independent of the CPU. The CPU can go on and do other things while the channel moves the data. Of course, before the CPU can *use* the data being moved in (input), or reuse the memory space occupied by data being moved out (output), it must wait for the channel to complete its task.

A number of schemes have been devised to speed up the overall process. On magnetic tape, information can be written very compactly. (Sixteen hundred characters per inch is typical, which means that the data on a punched card or from one line of a typical display terminal occupies only 0.05 inches. Some tapes can hold more than 6,000 characters per inch.) To read information from a tape, we must get the tape moving forward at full speed before we hit the first character of useful information, read the information, and come to a halt before we run into the next group of characters. This is accomplished by installing stretches of blank tape, called *inter-record gaps* (IRGs) between pieces of information. An IRG is about three-quarters of an inch in length (which is quite short considering that full speed for a tape drive is about 75 inches per second, 10 times faster than a home reel-to-reel tape recorder). The piece of information that lies between IRGs is called a *physical record* or *block*.

If we have only 80 characters of information in each block, a tape will consist mainly of blank space (0.75 inches of gap for each 0.05 inches of information at 1600 characters per inch). This is wasteful in two respects: To read 10 such records (half an inch of information) we have to bypass 7.5 inches of blank tape, which is time consuming and space wasting. In addition, we have to start up and stop the tape drive 10 times (make 10 *accesses*), which is even more time consuming.

A much better plan is to bunch several records together into a single block, surrounded by one set of IRGs. This process is called *blocking*. The amount of data we will be interested in at one time (in this case, 80 characters) is called a *logical record* (see Figure 7.13).

The way peripheral devices work, we must read (or write) an entire block at once. Consider input: If we have a blocking factor of 10 (i.e., 10 logical records per block), we will only access the tape every tenth time a record is needed. The first access actually moves 10 logical records into memory, into a temporary storage area called a *buffer*. When our program requests a record, a system program will hand it the next one from the buffer. When the buffer is exhausted, the system program signals the channel to bring the next block into the buffer.

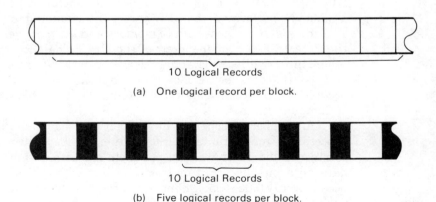

10 Logical Records

(a)   One logical record per block.

10 Logical Records

(b)   Five logical records per block.

FIGURE 7.13   Logical Records, Unblocked and Blocked

The shaded areas represent information from 80 character logical records, each occupying 0.05 inches of tape. The unshaded area surrounding information is the inter-record gap, occupying 0.75 inches.

	Not Blocked	10 Logical Records per Block
Space for data:	1000 records @ .05″ = 50″	1000 records @ .05″ = 50″
Space for IRGs:	1000 IRGs @ .75″ = 750″	100 IRGs @ .75″ = 75″
Total space:	800″ = ~67 feet	125″ = ~10 feet
# of Accesses	1000	100

FIGURE 7.14   Blocking

The table illustrates the dramatic savings in space and accesses that can be obtained by modest blocking. The figures shown are for 1000 80-character records, unblocked (i.e., one logical record per block) and blocked with a blocking factor of 10, at 1600 characters per inch.

Output works similarly: When our program says to write a logical record, the logical record is actually saved up in a buffer. The entire buffer is written onto tape as one block only after it is filled up with logical records. Any logical records remaining in the buffer when the program terminates are written out as a short block at the end of the tape. (This is called *flushing the buffer*.)

This is a great improvement over unblocked, unbuffered I/O (see Figure 7.14), but we can do better yet by using *two* buffers for each peripheral device. This new scheme is called *double buffering*. The problem in the previous scheme is that our program must still wait, twiddling its thumbs, while the buffer is being filled (input) or emptied (output). With two buffers, the program can work on one while the data channel works on the other.

For input, we instruct the channel to begin filling the first buffer at the very beginning of execution in the hope that, by the time we actually want to use information, it will already be moved into memory. Now, while we use the data in the first buffer, the channel fills the second buffer. We hope that by the time we are done with the data in the first buffer, the second buffer will be filled. (If not, we have to wait till it *is* filled.) Then we go on to use the information in the second buffer while the channel refills the first buffer. And so on.

On output, we place information into the first buffer. When it is full, we signal the data channel to begin writing it out while we go on to fill the second buffer. We hope that by the time we are done filling the second buffer, the first buffer will have been emptied by the channel. (If not, we have to wait.) Then we go on to refill the first buffer while the channel is emptying the second. And so on.

Note that input double buffering is exactly the same as output double buffering except that the channel and CPU have swapped roles. (See Figure 7.15.)

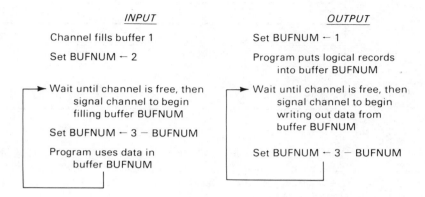

INPUT

Channel fills buffer 1

Set BUFNUM ← 2

→ Wait until channel is free, then
    signal channel to begin
    filling buffer BUFNUM

Set BUFNUM ← 3 − BUFNUM

Program uses data in
buffer BUFNUM

OUTPUT

Set BUFNUM ← 1

Program puts logical records
into buffer BUFNUM

→ Wait until channel is free, then
    signal channel to begin
    writing out data from
    buffer BUFNUM

Set BUFNUM ← 3 − BUFNUM

FIGURE 7.15   Double Buffering

EXERCISES

Terms You Should Know . . .

Block	Inter-Record Gap
Buffer	Logical Record
Complete Inversion	Logical Sequential Organization
Data Channel	Longitudinal Check Character
Data Item	Parity Track
Direct Access Device	Partial Inversion
Directory	Physical Record
Disk	Random Organization
Double Buffering	Record
Drum	Rotational Delay
Error Correcting	Seek
Error Detecting	Sequential Device
File	Sequential Organization
Indexed Organization	Unit Record Device

1. What kind of storage device *is* a jukebox?

2. Why is it necessary to rewrite a sequential file when it is being updated?

3. Suggest how a file with an alphabetic key can be accessed by a multilevel directory of an arbitrarily large number of parts.

4. Devise an algorithm (or sketch a method) by which an indexed file *with overflow records* can be read sequentially.

5. What is the disadvantage of eliminating the data value from records in a linked list, even when presence on the list implies the value. (For example, when we have separate lists of the math majors, the chemistry majors, etc.)

6. Find the bit in error in Figure 7.12 (b).

7. It is at least imaginable to have a magnetic tape with multiple parity tracks (or, more generally, error detection tracks). Taking something of an extreme, we could even imagine every track appearing twice (or each character appearing twice) with a checking mechanism that makes sure that the two versions are really identical. Discuss the advantages and disadvantages of such a scheme.

8. Reconstruct Figure 7.14, this time using 10,000 records of 120 characters each, unblocked vs. a blocking factor of 100 records per block.

9. Describe the process that adds a record to a system in which all of the record's 20 fields are inverted.

PART 3: REFERENCES

1. Climenson, W. D. "File Organization and Search Techniques." In C. A. Cuadra (Ed.), *Annual Review of Information Science and Technology*. New York: Wiley, 1966.

2. Dewar, R. B. K. *Use of Computers in X-Ray Phase Problems*. Doctoral Dissertation (Department of Chemistry), University of Chicago, 1968.

3. Dodd, G. G. "Elements of Data Management Systems." *ACM Computing Surveys*, 1 (2), June 1969, pp. 117–133.

4. Flores, I. "Computer Time for Address Calculation Sorting." *Journal of the ACM*, 8, 1969, pp. 389–409.

5. Floyd, R. W. "Algorithm 245, TREESORT3." *Communications of the ACM*, 7 (12), December, 1964, p. 701.

6. Gottlieb, C. C. "Sorting on Computers." *Communications of the ACM*, 6 (5), May 1963, pp. 194–201.

7. Knuth, D. E., *The Art of Computer Programming*. Vol. 1: Fundamental Algorithms (Chapter 2, "Information Structures"); Vol. 3: Sorting and Searching. Reading MA: Addison-Wesley, 1968; 1973.

INDEX